MILITARY
MEMOIRS
OF
MR. GEORGE THOMAS

MILITARY

MEMOIRS

OF

MR. GEORGE THOMAS

WHO,

By extraordinary Talents and Enterprize,

ROSE FROM AN OBSCURE SITUATION TO THE RANK OF

A GENERAL,

IN THE SERVICE OF THE NATIVE POWERS

IN THE

NORTH-WEST OF INDIA.

WILLIAM FRANCKLIN

GYAN

Published by

GYAN

Gyan Publishing House
5, Ansari Road
Daryaganj, New Delhi-110002
Phone: 011-47034999, 9811692060
E-mail: books@gyanbooks.com

Distribution Network
gyanbooks.com
India, USA, Canada, UK, Australia, France

ISBN : 978-81-212-9510-9 (PB)
First Published, 1805

2nd Impression 2023

Printed at: Gyan Press, Delhi.

MILITARY MEMOIRS OF MR. GEORGE THOMAS
Author: WILLIAM FRANCKLIN

GENERAL GEORGE THOMAS.

Obit August 1802 Ætat 46

Published 10th Sept.r 1805, by J. Stockdale Piccadilly.

MILITARY

MEMOIRS

OF

MR. GEORGE THOMAS;

WHO,

By extraordinary Talents and Enterprize,

ROSE FROM AN OBSCURE SITUATION TO THE RANK OF

A GENERAL,

IN THE SERVICE OF THE NATIVE POWERS

IN THE

NORTH-WEST OF INDIA.

THROUGH THE WORK ARE INTERSPERSED,
Geographical and Statiſtical Accounts of ſeveral of the States compoſing the Interior of the Peninſula, eſpecially the Countries of Jypoor, Joudpoor, and Oudipoor, by Geographers denominated Rajpootaneh, the Seiks of Punjaub, the Territory of Beykaneer, and the Country adjoining the Great Deſart to the weſtward of Hurrianeh.

COMPILED AND ARRANGED FROM
MR. THOMAS'S ORIGINAL DOCUMENTS.

BY WILLIAM FRANCKLIN.

CAPTAIN OF INFANTRY;
Member of the Asiatic Society, Author of a Tour to Persia, and of the History of Shah Aulum.

—— MORES, POPULOS, ET PRÆLIA DICAM.

1805.

LIST OF PLATES.

CONTENTS.

CHAP. I.

CHAP. II.

CHAP. III.

CHAP. IV.

CHAP. V.

CHAP. VI.

CHAP. VII.

CHAP. VIII.

CHAP. IX.

CONTENTS.

CHAP. XIV.

MEMOIRS

OF

GEORGE THOMAS.

CHAPTER I.

Introduction.—Mr. Thomas enters into the ſervice of Appakandarow,—Repairs to Delhi.—Account of the environs of that city.

IN the enlightened period of the nineteenth century, when the world abounds in characters, as diſtinguiſhed for their abilities, in every branch of ſcientific and uſeful knowledge, as eminent for their courage and other perſonal qualifications, it may afford matter for ſurpriſe, that an obſcure individual ſhould merit the attention of the community. Yet, when it is conſidered that the ſingularity of character, exhibited in the ſubject of the preſent memoirs, is rendered ſtill more intereſting by his adventures, his talents, his ſucceſſes, and his misfortunes, detailed in the following ſheets, it may not only form the beſt apology for the compiler in ſubmitting theſe memoirs to the public view, but alſo afford ſome uſeful inſtruction to the reader.

From the beſt information we could procure, it appears that Mr. George Thomas firſt came to India in a Britiſh ſhip of war, in 1781-2. His ſituation in the fleet was humble, having ſerved as a quarter maſter, or, as is affirmed by ſome, in the capacity of a common ſailor.

Shortly after landing in the vicinity of Madras, the activity of his mind, overcoming the lowlineſs of his ſituation, he determined to quit the ſhip, and embrace a life more ſuitable to his ardent diſpoſition.

His firſt ſervice was among the Polygars to the ſouthward, where he reſided a few years. But at length ſetting out over-land, he ſpiritedly traverſed the central part of the Peninſula, and about the year 1787 arrived at Delhi. Here he received a commiſſion in the ſervice of the Begum Sumroo. This lady is well known in the hiſtory of the tranſactions of modern times. Soon after his arrival at Delhi, the Begum, with her uſual judgment and diſcrimination of character, advanced him to a command in her army. From this period his military career in the north-weſt of India may be ſaid to have commenced.

In various and ſucceſſive actions againſt the Seiks, and others of the Begum's enemies, Mr. Thomas, by his courage and perſeverance, rendered her authority reſpectable. By theſe ſucceſſes, he obtained a conſiderable influence over the mind of his miſtreſs, and was for ſome time her chief adviſer and counſellor.*

* Among other brilliant acts, performed by Mr. Thomas, during his service with the Begum, was the circumstance related in the History of Shah Aulum. The Compiler of these Memoirs did not know, at the time, that Mr. Thomas was the officer who commanded the party. But that gentleman, during his residence at Benares, communi-

But, unfortunately for the mutual interests of both parties, after a residence of six or seven years, Mr. Thomas had the mortification to find himself supplanted in the good opinion of the Begum. His authority was assumed by a more successful rival.

This conduct in the Begum, exciting much animosity and many heart-burnings between the two rival commanders, Mr. Thomas resolved to embark his fortunes on a different service. He therefore quitted the Begum Sumroo, and about 1792 betook himself to the frontier station of the British army, at the post of Anopshire.

Here he waited several months, in the expectation of receiving overtures for employment from some of the native powers. He was not deceived in these expectations. In the beginning of the year 1793, Mr. Thomas, being at Anopshire, received letters from Ap-

rated a detail of the affair, which, with a slight variation in a few particulars, happened as is stated in the printed work. See the History of Shah Aulum, page 167, et seq.

pakandarow, a Mahratta chief, conveying offers of ſervice, and promiſes of a comfortable proviſion.

To comprehend the nature and uſe of Mr. Thomas's ſervices at that juncture, it will be neceſſary to recur to the previous ſituation and proſpects of Appakandarow.

This chief had formerly been himſelf in the ſervice of Madhajee Scindiah, who gave him the command of two battalions of infantry, raiſed and diſciplined by the celebrated General Duboigne. In return for Appakandarow's ſervices, Scindiah had alſo, ſubſequently, entruſted to his management the diſtricts of Gualier and Gohud. Theſe, for ſome time, he conducted with ſucceſs: but having, in the year 1790, invaded Bundelcund, and being unſucceſsful in his operations, he was compelled to contract debts to a conſiderable amount. This irregular and improvident conduct occaſioned, firſt, his removal from command, and afterwards, his diſmiſſion from Scindiah's employ. Of a haughty and impatient ſpirit, Appakandarow ill brooked this humiliation, and from that time ſought, by his own exertion, to eſtabliſh an independency. It was at this period he was joined by Mr. Thomas, who had with him 250 cavalry, choſen men, and of tried valour on ſeveral occaſions.

This acceſſion of force was highly acceptable to the Mahratta chief; he was, at that time, unable to keep under ſubjection ſeveral diſtricts, which, on account of his ill ſucceſs, had rebelled againſt his authority, and withheld the payment of their accuſtomed tribute.

Mr. Thomas was now directed by Appakandarow to raiſe a battalion conſiſting of 1000 men and 100 cavalry. For the maintenance of this force, he aſſigned to him the pergunnas of Thajara, Thopookara, and Ferozeepoor. They are all in the Mawatty diſtrict, ſituated to the ſouth-weſt of Delhi. Thoſe diſtricts had, ſome years preceding, been in a ſtate of rebellion, nor was Appakandarow able to reduce them to ſubmiſſion. The inhabitants, when a large force was ſent againſt them, uſually took ſhelter in the mountains;

but when the force was inferior in numbers, by uniting, they proved victorious. With cavalry, likewise, they committed depredations in every direction. These excesses naturally rendered the Mahratta chief anxious of transferring the districts to any person who would exert himself to prevent their plundering the industrious peasants. Mr. Thomas's agreement with Appakandarow was, that he should balance accounts every six months. These terms having been agreed on, as an assurance of confidence, he presented Mr. Thomas with two guns, some ammunition, and a few bullocks.

The necessary arrangements having been made, Mr. Thomas prepared to march, and take possession of the lands aforementioned. He was however stopped by accounts, dispatched by Mr. Perron, announcing the death of Scindiah.

The march thus postponed, Appakandarow repaired to Delhi to guard against an apprehended commotion in that capital. On their arrival at court, Appakandarow, and other chiefs, among whom was Mr. Thomas, were honoured with Khilluts, similar presents were likewise given for Dowlut Row Scindiah, who had now succeeded to the possessions of his deceased uncle.

The mention of Delhi affords an opportunity of presenting the reader with an account of some remarkable buildings, which stand without the precincts of the new city, and have hitherto escaped the observation of travellers. They were obtained by the compiler of these Memoirs during a visit to this celebrated city, in 1793.

We come next to the tomb of Humaioon, the son of Baber, second of the imperial House of Timoor, and memorable for a chequered life of alternate prosperity and misfortune.— He died Anno Hejirah 963, and the mausoleum was erected by his son, the famous Akbar, on the western bank of the Jumna, in the city of old Delhi.

The building is situated in the centre of an

ample terrace, of red ſtone, two thouſand feet in circumference.

Upon this terrace riſes the mauſoleum of ſolid red ſtone. It is of a circular form, ſurmounted by a ſtupendous dome of white marble. Conſpicuous from its dimenſions, this dome is ſeen at a great diſtance. Four minarets, of red and white marble, ſupport the extremities of the building. Theſe are crowned with octagon pavilions of red ſtone, having marble cupolas. I judge the height to be about a hundred and twenty feet. A winding ſtair-caſe, of red ſtone, leads to a terrace, which encircles the exterior of the dome; hence you have a noble proſpect, both of the old and new Delhi.

The principal room below, is paved with large ſlabs of white marble. It contains the ſepulchre of Humaioon, of the common ſize, but elegantly decorated with chiſel work: it bears no inſcription. Adjoining to this room, are other apartments, in which are interred ſeveral princeſſes of the Houſe of Timoor.

Upon the terrace aforementioned are the graves of five princes of the royal family, viz, Darah Shekoah, who was put to death by order of his brother Aurungzebe. 2d. Mooizaddeen or, Jehandar. 3d. Shah Furrukſeir, put to death by the Seyuds. 4th. Beedar Bukht. 5th. Azim Shah, ſon of Aurungzebe. Near them is the grave of the late Emperor, the ſecond Aulumgeer.

About two hundred yards from the mauſoleum of Humaioon, is that of the famous Khan Khanan, prime miniſter of Jehangeer, and ſon of the renowned Byram Khan, memorable for contributing, in ſo great a degree, during the ſucceſſive reigns of Humaioon, Akbar, and Jehangeer, to eſtabliſh the Houſe of Timoor on the throne of Hindoſtan. The tomb reſembles, both in ſhape and ſize, that of the Nawaub Sufdar Jung. The fine marble covering however of the dome, as well as the inlayings of the minarets, and the gateways, have been dilapidated.

The generous mind cannot without indignation perceive the ravages which the different invaders of Hindoſtan have perpetrated upon theſe magnificent remains of departed grandeur. But what ſhall we ſay of thoſe now living* who, for the paltry conſideration of a few thouſand rupees, ſtrip the venerable ſhrines of the ſervants of their departed anceſtors, and, by robbing the dead of what gratitude or affection had beſtowed as a parting teſtimony, acquire thereby a partial, and diſgraceful opulence?

A mile to the ſouthward of the new city are the remains of the fort, palace, and moſque of the Patan emperor, the firſt Feroze. Theſe ruins embrace a conſiderable extent. The walls of the fort are of immenſe thickneſs, and the prodigious quantity of granite, with other ſtones, ſpread in heaps over the whole of the interior of the incloſure, denote it to have been a grand and ſplendid edifice.

This fort was built Anno Hejirah 755, and was deſtroyed by the Mogul conqueror Timoor,

* To every one at Delhi, it is notorious that a Prince of the House of Timoor now living, has actually sold the marble of this tomb, for twenty five thousand rupees.

in his invaſion of Hindoſtan. Toward the centre of the place is a building of an ancient ſtyle, flanked with round pillars, and crowned with turrets of three ſtories. At the top of this building, on an ample terrace of ſtone, about forty feet in height, is a column of brown granite. On this column is an inſcription, in the ancient character beforementioned, as diſcernible on the pillar in the fort of Allahabad, and compoſed of the ſame materials. This pillar is called, by the natives, *Feroze Cotelah*, the ſtaff of Feroze, and from the conſtruction of the building on which it is placed, I ſhould conjecture it has been a monument of Hindoo grandeur, prior to the irruptions of the Muſſulmans. Adjoining to the cotelah, is a very large building differing in the ſtyle of its architecture from thoſe moſques built ſubſequent to the eſtabliſhment of the Moguls. This moſque is ſquare, has four extenſive aiſles or cloiſters, the roofs of which are ſtone, and ſupported by two hundred and fifty columns of ſtone, about ſixteen feet high. The length of the cloiſters gives a grand appearance to the building. An octangular dome, of ſtone and brick work, about twenty-five feet high, rises from the centre of the mosque. In the western cloister is a kibla, or niche, in the wall, in the direction of Mecca. Of this mosque the emperor Timoor took a model, and carrying it with him on his return to Samarcand his capital, accompanied at the same time by artificers and workmen of every description, he shortly after his arrival built a magnificent temple.

In the northern aisle of this mosque, at the upper end, is a small window, from which was thrown the body of the late emperor the second Allumgeer, who had been assassinated at the instigation of his vizier Gaziodeen Khan. The assassins were two Mahomedan devotees, whom he had visited under the pretext of their working miracles. The body of this unfortunate prince, unburied, for two days lay on the sands of the Jumna. At last it was taken up by permission of Gaziodeen, and interred in the sepulchre of Humaioon. To me it appears that the style of building in this mosque, refers to a period in the architecture of Hindostan prior to the Mogul conquests. The mosque at Paniput, erected by the emperor Baber, may be looked upon as the model of all the ſucceeding Mogul buildings.

COOTTUB MINÂR.

Nine miles ſouth of Delhi is the celebrated column, deſignated Coottub Minar, ſituated near, and deriving that name from the tomb of Khaja Cuttubadeen. His diſciple, Shemſadeen, of the family of Ghazi, erected this column, Anno Hejirah 770. Shemſadeen deſigned that this pillar and another ſimilar one ſhould have marked the entrance of a magnificent moſque. It was begun upon the ruins of a Hindoo temple. Having finiſhed this pillar, and parts of the buildings adjacent, Shemſadeen's premature death prevented the completion of a work which would have been one of the moſt magnificent in the world. The whole was intended as a monument to perpetuate to poſterity the triumph of Mahomedan faith over that of Brimha. The column has a moſt ſtupendous appearance. Conceive a ſhaft of ſixty feet diameter, compoſed partly of red ſtone, partly of white marble, riſing to the height of two hundred and fifty feet.

Aſcending this pillar, relief is afforded by four projecting galleries of red ſtone. Tapering toward the ſummit, it was crowned with an octagon pavilion. I imagine this pavilion would have contained at leaſt, a dozen perſons. Each of the galleries are moſt richly tho' differently ornamented. The column is relieved, and rendered ſtrikingly bold, by convex and angular projections.

Within this grand tower, is a circular ſtaircaſe of three hundred and eight ſteps of red ſtone. There are, at intervals, landing places which communicate with windows. From the octagon, on the ſummit, the view is ſtrikingly grand. Looking from ſuch a height, the mind is impreſſed with ſenſations of admiration and of awe. Inſcriptions in ſeveral parts, twelve inches in breadth, embrace the column. Theſe contain verſes from the Koran, in the Arabick character. The galleries are ſupported by ſculptured ornaments.

of which the richneſs is greatly heightened by a profuſion of frieze work.

This deſcription of the Coottub Minar, with the engraving* ſhewing the veſtiges of the ruins which ſurround it, will I doubt not incline the reader to think with me that they are objects to a traveller, perhaps, equally intereſting as any in the world; and through the eaſt are not to be found more impreſſive memorials of its ingenuity, its magnificence, and its grandeur.

*. For this I am indebted to the kindness of Lieutenant Macdougal, of the engineers, from whose sketch, on the spot, it has been engraved.

S.W. VIEW OF THE COOTUB MINAR.

Height of the Column 250 feet, Diameter 60 d°.

CHAPTER II.

Mr. Thomas marches towards his new Pergunnahs.—Military operations.—Intrigues of Begum Somroo.—She is depoſed.—Death of Levaſſo.—Altercation betwixt Mr. Thomas and Appakandarow.—Occurrences.

HAVING remained ſome time at Delhi, it afforded Mr. Thomas the opportunity of recruiting his forces to 700 men; with this reinforcement, he prepared for his departure to the diſtricts which had been aſſigned to him by Appakandarow.

To the accompliſhment of that purpoſe a new obſtacle aroſe;—unable to pay his troops, they became mutinous, and plundered the adjacent country. This conduct diſguſting Appakandarow, produced high words between him and Mr. Thomas. The diſpute, after much altercation, ended in a compromiſe, by which Mr. Thomas received the ſum of 14,000 rupees, and an aſſignment for the reſt of his claims. The latter, however, was never fulfilled.

In the march towards his diſtricts, Mr. Thomas retaliated upon the Begum Sumroo, whom he now conſidered his bitter enemy, laying under contribution that part of her country which came within his route.

Arriving at Goorath, a large and populous village, he impoſed heavy contributions. Theſe amounted to a conſiderable ſum. He found here alſo an ample ſupply of bullocks and forage.

Continuing his march, after a long and tedious day's journey, he encamped near the town of Tejara, a place in the centre of the Mewattee diſtrict. The night was dark and rainy: this and the extreme fatigue of the ſoldiers conſpired to render ſucceſsful an attempt which the Mewattys made, and they carried off a horſe from the very centre of the camp.

In the morning, a party was detached to discover the village to which the horſe had been conveyed. The party had not proceeded far when they were attacked, and obliged to retreat. Orders were then given for the cavalry to advance, and cover the detachment. And Mr. Thomas himſelf leading the infantry, haſtily marched, and with his collected force, attacked the enemy at the village, to which, it appears, the horſe had been carried. By this time they had aſſembled and became formidable. The centre diviſion of Mr. Thomas's troops, in a ſhort time ſet fire to the village, and there ſeemed no doubt of a complete victory, when the diviſions on the right and left giving way, fled with precipitation. The wounded left on the field were, even at this criſis of the action, cut to pieces by the enemy.

The centre diviſion, under the ſpecial command of Mr. Thomas, now following the example of their brethren, left him, of his troops, only a dozen infantry and a few cavalry.

Thus diſcomfited and vexed by the unſteadineſs of his troops, Mr. Thomas, as a laſt reſort, encouraged his ſmall party to exert themſelves in extricating a nine-pounder, which unfortunately, previouſly to the battle, had ſtuck in the bed of a nullah. In this he had juſt ſucceeded, when the enemy, as certain of victory, recommenced a furious attack, and endeavoured to ſeize the gun.

The commandant of cavalry, a man of diſtinguiſhed bravery, ſtill adhered to Mr. Thomas, and deſperately, with a few others, threw himſelf between the gun and the enemy. *They* were cut to pieces, but the gallant effort afforded time to re-mount and oppoſe a well-directed fire of grape from the nine-pounder. This ſaved Mr. Thomas and the brave few of his ſurviving party. For, after the diſcharge of a few rounds, the enemy retired to the ſurrounding ravines.

Mr. Thomas now collected the fugitives, who with his veteran party formed a detachment of about 300 men. With theſe he unconcernedly challenged the enemy to a renewal of the combat, which they now as cautiouſly declined.

In its firſt view ſo diſaſtrous, this action, by the dread it ſpread among the enemy, proved highly fortunate. Great as was Mr. Thomas's loſs of brave and attached ſoldiers, that of the Mewattys was infinitely more conſiderable. The immediate conſequence was an overture, on the part of their chief, of terms which ſhortly led to an amicable adjuſtment. They agreed to pay Mr. Thomas a year's rent, and to reſtore to him the property that had been ſtolen. The performance of theſe articles was guaranteed by ſecurities.

The puniſhment of this village, the ſtrongeſt in the whole diſtrict, and its inhabitants the moſt refractory, was highly favourable to Mr. Thomas's intereſt; the more ſo, as in a preceding campaign the whole force of Begum Sumroo had been in vain exerted to reduce it. Mr. Thomas next prepared to march againſt the remaining diſtricts which were ſtill in rebellion; and, having recruited his force for this purpoſe, he was ordered by Appakandarow to aſſiſt the collector of the diſtrict of Kiſhnagur.

Convinced by experience that vigorous meaſures could alone enſure ſucceſs, Mr. Thomas marched towards the refractory villages; of which having gained poſſeſſion, they were quickly conſumed by fire.

An example ſo ſevere deterred others from purſuing a ſimilar conduct. Of theſe the moſt conſiderable was the town of Jyjur; which, however, ſubmitting on the approach of the troops, oppoſition was at an end, and Mr. Thomas returned to Tejara.

On the ſubmiſſion of Jyjur, Appakandarow gave Mr. Thomas an order for a ſupply of money upon the collector of that place. The collector endeavoured to evade payment, by repreſenting that the diſtreſſed ſituation of Appakandarow (whoſe troops had juſt mutinied for want of payment of their arrears), required every rupee that could be raiſed; in conſequence, Mr. Thomas muſt, for the preſent, diſpenſe with payment. This, he obſerves, was true; but his people being in diſtreſs, to provide a remedy, he marched to Behadurghur, in order to raise by contribution the necessary supplies.

In his route, the small villages were found to be deserted and the large ones increased with numbers of armed persons. By this time, Mr. Thomas's troops, thinned by frequent desertions, amounted only to 300 men; but these, had they been soldiers accustomed to discipline, would still have been sufficient to answer the purpose of completing the reduction of the rebellious Zemindars.

Arriving at Mundaka, the Zemindars of which place had been the original cause of the misunderstanding betwixt Appakandarow and Mr. Thomas, were found ready for the combat; Mr. Thomas therefore, though with a force so inconsiderable, hesitated not in making an immediate attack: in this he was successful, and having defeated the enemy, he found in the place plunder to the amount of four thousand rupees.

During these transactions, the Begum Sumroo, and the Mahratta governor of Delhi, jealous of the aſcendancy Mr. Thomas had acquired, ſent a force to watch his motions: for the preſent he thought the moſt prudent method to eſcape obſervation would be by removing to a diſtance, and his new levies being now complete, he marched directly back to the town of Tejara.

At this place Mr. Thomas received a letter from Appakandarow, who was ſtill detained in the fort of Kotepootly by the mutinous ſtate of his troops. His ſituation had been rendered thus unpleaſant by the intrigues of Gopaul Row, Scindia's commander in chief. That chief had written letters to the principal ſirdars in the army, promiſing them payment of their arrears provided they would deliver up Appa as a priſoner. He further obſerved, that he had but too much reaſon to imagine the ſirdars would yield a ready acquieſcence to this offer; that, diſtreſſed for proviſions, and having his family with him, if Mr. Thomas could not come to his aſſiſtance, he muſt ultimately be compelled to throw himſelf on the mercy of his enemies.

On receipt of this letter, although it rained heavily and the day was far advanced, Mr. Thomas, without hesitation, set off: he marched all that night and the best part of the ensuing day and night through a constant and heavy rain. About two o'clock in the morning he arrived at the fort of Kotepootly. The incessant rain prevented his having any opposition from the enemy without, and he encamped under the walls of the fort. The communication was thus happily opened, and provisions being sent in, plenty succeeded to the scarcity before experienced.

Mr. Thomas, aware that the force of the mutineers would daily become augmented, recommended to Appakandarow to evacuate the fort, and retreat to Kanoond. In the mean time he advised that letters should be written to Scindia, to deprecate the resentment of that chief. Approving of Mr. Thomas's proposal, Appakandarow appointed the ensuing day for the accomplishment of his purpose, and the business was conducted with so much secresy and address, that until the moment of departure every one seemed ignorant of the intended movement. At the appointed hour, Appakandarow, attended by a few persons who still adhered to him, came out of the fort of Kotepootly with his family and effects; he was received by Mr. Thomas, and placed in the centre of a strong detachment, who formed around him, and commenced their march.

In order to protect the baggage, Mr. Thomas, with the remainder of his force, remained behind for a short time, but the enemy now appearing prepared to pursue the detachment with determination to rescue Appakandarow, Mr. Thomas, without further delay, joined that chief. They had not proceeded far when the van of the enemy made their appearance: Mr. Thomas, as the only means of inspiring confidence, recommended to Appakandarow to mount an elephant, and shew himself to the troops. The measure was instantly adopted, and attended with the happiest effect; for the enemy perceiving this resolute conduct thought it most prudent to retire, and Mr. Thomas, without further opposition, conducted his chief in safety to Kanoond. Appakandarow, released from his embarrassment, was desirous of making a grateful return for the ſervices that had been rendered. He adopted Mr. Thomas as his ſon, preſented him with the ſum of three thouſand rupees to purchaſe an elephant and palankeen ſuitable to the dignity of his ſtation, ordered him to encreaſe his force two hundred infantry and as many cavalry; and finally, made over to him, in perpetuity, the diſtricts of Jyjur, Byree, Mandoté, and Phatoda, which yield an annual revenue of a lack and fifty thouſand rupees.

He was then diſmiſſed by Appakandarow, and directed to complete the arrangement of the remaining diſtricts in the Mewatty country.

This was become more neceſſary; a principal Zemindar, by name Gunga Biſhen, and of the tribe called Aheer,* had not only openly rebelled, but had made offers to Gopaul Row of ſurrendering up the diſtrict to Scindia; as an additional inducement for his acceptance,

* This tribe can bring into the field a body of fourteen thousand men.

the rebel ſtated that the real amount of the revenues were much larger than what had been acknowledged by Appakandarow, and paid by him to Scindia as his lord paramount. Appa being appriſed of this treacherous correspondence, directed Mr. Thomas without delay to march and attack the rebel. He, on diſcloſure of his treachery, fled to the mountainous part of the Mewatty country, and there fortified himſelf. The orders for the march had been kept a profound ſecret in Mr. Thomas's camp. Arriving ſuddenly before the place, by a ſucceſsful ſtratagem Mr. Thomas took Gunga Biſhen priſoner, whom he ſent to Appa. The fort was ſtill maintained by his nephew, and a garriſon of one thouſand men; they had abundance of proviſions, ammunition, and ſtores of all kinds; the only inconvenience ſuſtained by the inhabitants was a ſcarcity of water. This article was not to be procured within two miles of the place. Mr. Thomas, in the hope of compelling them to ſurrender, commenced a blockade; and the better to enſure ſucceſs he conſtructed a chain of redoubts round the fort.

Whilst employed in the erection of these posts he had a narrow escape for his life. Retired to snatch an hour of sleep and refreshment from the toils of the preceding day, Mr. Thomas was suddenly awakened in the night by the noise and shouts of the enemy. Repairing to an eminence in the neighbourhood, he had the mortification to perceive that his own people had given way, and the enemy were become masters of a newly-finished redoubt, together with the arms and ammunition contained within: to add to his distress he perceived a party advancing to the place where he stood, unarmed and defenceless, (the hurry of his being awoke not giving him time to secure either pistols or side-arms): fortunately however for him, a faithful servant had followed him with his sword, which taking from the man's hand he prepared for his defence.

From various quarters spears were thrown, and matchlocks fired at him but without effect. Perceiving a stand of colours which his own men had left behind, he stooped to pick them up, which the enemy observing, concluded by the motion of his body that he had been wounded; they rushed on him in numbers, and wounded him in several places. This compelled him to relinquish the colours and attack the enemy, whom he soon obliged to retreat. Mr. Thomas then ascended an eminence, in order to discover, if possible, the direction his own troops had taken in their pusillanimous flight, but in vain. Faint from the wounds he had received in the late encounter, he now retired within his trenches and got them dressed. The siege of the place advanced apace, and two mines having been sprung with considerable effect the garrison capitulated.

During this siege Mr. Thomas and his people had undergone great hardship. Whilst the grain remained on the ground he was enabled to procure supplies from the neighbouring country, but the harvest being got in they were reduced to a scarcity of provisions. His own tent, the only one in the camp, was converted into an hospital for the sick and wounded; and the season being severe Mr. Thomas humanely sold his own horses to procure blankets for the men.

Mr. Thomas next marched to Jyjur: on his arrival at that place, the zemindars who had revolted, not chusing to contest the point, paid their rents, and the troops received their arrears.

Gopaul Row, the Mahratta general, was about this time superseded in his office of lieutenant-general of the possessions of Scindia in Hindostan. Luckwah Dadah and Jigwah Bapoo were appointed to succeed him. In this state of Mr. Thomas's affairs, the army of these chiefs arrived in the vicinity of Appa's country. That chief determined to pay his respects, and for this purpose repaired to their camp; at first he was well received, but had not long remained when a sum of money was required of him under pretext of payment of an old tribute due to Scindia. He was moreover informed, that until this was paid he would be detained in the camp.

Unable to raise the sum demanded, Appakandarow was under the necessity of resigning the best part of his country into the hands of Bapoo Farnevese, who had been appointed by the expreſs orders of the Poona government. Although the ſum required was leſs than two lacks of rupees, and many perſons in Appa's family could eaſily have afforded him aſſiſtance in his diſtreſs, not a man was to be found who would now part with a rupee. The diſtricts were therefore made over in mortgage; and the ſum required by the Mahratta commanders was advanced by Bapoo Farneveſe.

It was moreover ſtipulated, that the troops kept up by Bapoo, for the purpoſe of collection, ſhould be paid from the treaſury of Appakandarow. " In ſhort (ſays Mr. Thomas in terms of indignation) it was plainly to be ſeen, that whoever might hereafter, by chance of war, obtain poſſeſſion of the diſtricts in queſtion, it was evident that by theſe conceſſions, Appa had for ever done away his own right."

Among theſe pergunnahs were three in the Mewatty country which belonged to Mr. Thomas. The loſs to him was ſevere; but, as he obſerves with a conſideration highly to his credit as a ſoldier, " I had no cauſe for

" complaint when my principal was ruined." After theſe tranſactions Mr. Thomas was directed to aſſiſt the deputy appointed by Appa to collect the revenues of the remaining part of his country: a taſk of conſiderable difficulty; ſince the Zemindars, hearing of Appa's detention in the camp of the Mahrattas, had broken out into open rebellion againſt his authority. To reduce them to obedience, Mr. Thomas marched with about eight hundred men that remained after the heavy ſervice he had lately experienced; promptitude in planning, and vigour in execution, being abſolutely neceſſary, Mr. Thomas, by his animated exertions, in a very ſhort time captured ſeveral of the principal places, ſome by day aſſaults, and others by night.

Among others, the capture of Byree appears intereſting in the narration. " In the fort, ſays Mr. Thomas, " excluſive of the garriſon, " were three hundred rajepoots and jauts. " Theſe had been hired for the expreſs pur- " poſe of defending the place, and it was here " I was in the moſt imminent danger of loſing " the whole of my party. We had ſtormed

" the fort, and were beat back with loſs;
" one of my ſirdars was wounded, and, from
" the confuſion that occurred, left behind in
" the hands of the enemy; the danger was
" every moment increaſing, the town was on
" fire in ſeveral parts, and our retreat nearly
" cut off by the flames that ſurrounded us.

"In this ſituation, we had the additional
" mortification to perceive the mercileſs enemy
" ſeize on the wounded officer, and, with ſa-
" vage barbarity, precipitate him into the fire.
" Equally animated, as enraged, by this ſpec-
" tacle, my troops now ruſhed forward to the
" attack, with an ardour that was irreſiſtible.
" Having gained entire poſſeſſion of the fort,
" the ſoldiers, with clamorous expreſſions of re-
" venge, inſiſted on the death of every one of
" the garriſon that remained, and I was not in-
" clined to refuſe; but it coſt us dear, the
" enemy to a man made a brave reſiſtance.
" This conteſt was continued ſo long, as to
" afford time to thoſe who had retreated, to
" return: by this means, we were again en-
" gaged, and at one time almoſt overpowered;
" but, receiving a reinforcement of our own

"party, the enemy, by ſlow degrees, began "again to retreat which they effected. I "purſued with the cavalry: the enemy once "more made a ſtand in the jungles adjoining "to the town; when, after a ſecond deſperate "conflict, they gave way on all ſides, and "moſt of them were cut to pieces."

Scarcely however had Mr. Thomas completed the objects of his march, when he received letters from Appa, of a tendency moſt unpromiſing: in theſe, Appa, after deſcanting on his finances, the low ſtate of which did not permit him to retain longer, either Mr. Thomas or his troops, recommended him to diſmiſs his battalions, and repair to the head quarters, which were now in the country of the Row Rajah.

In anſwer, Mr. Thomas ſtated his utter impoſſibility to diſcharge the men, without previous payment of their arrears. He then marched to join Appa, and found that chief in the vicinity of Alwar. Appa, after expatiating on the ungrateful conduct of thoſe perſons who had enjoyed his confidence, informed Mr.

Thomas, in terms of apparent uneasiness, that the Mahratta commanders, who had become acquainted with his influence, and the part he had taken in the business against the mutineers, considered him as a dangerous person; as one who would, if occasion occurred, act against the interests of Scindia himself: they had therefore requested of him to discharge Mr. Thomas from the service.

This information, however, Mr. Thomas found to be incorrect; for in a conference he had with Luckwa on the following day, that chief not only disclaimed all idea of disapproving Mr. Thomas's conduct, but even offered him the command of two thousand men in the service of Scindia.

Mr. Thomas, for several reasons, declined closing with this proposal. The districts of Appa's country were now in open rebellion; and, notwithstanding the present deceit on his part, Mr. Thomas considered himself under obligations which could not be passed over; that if he now quitted him, it would in all probability prove his utter ruin; he therefore resolved to adhere to Appakandarow, and endeavour to retrieve his affairs.

Appa excuſed himſelf for his late conduct, and Mr. Thomas now prepared for his march. For the preſent he was interrupted by a requeſt from Luckwa to afford his aſſiſtance in the reduction of a fort which had refuſed to pay the uſual tribute. Mr. Thomas, with the conſent of Appa, joined the forces of Luckwa, and commenced their march.

On their arrival before the place Mr. Thomas's poſt was aſſigned him; but his ſoldiers being now ſix months in arrears, refuſed, without payment, to proceed: in this exigency, Mr. Thomas, to ſatisfy their demands, was once more compelled to part with his property; having done this, the ſoldiers returned to their duty.

The enemy, in the hope of compelling the Mahrattas to raiſe the ſiege, had taken poſſeſſion of the ravines in the neighbourhood: ſeveral ſkirmiſhes took place, with loſs on both ſides.

A propoſal was made by Mr. Gardiner, the commandant of a brigade of Scindia's troops, to advance the ſecond parallel: a council aſſembled to conſult on the moſt eligible mode, but finding this could not be effected without firſt taking a redoubt which lay in their front, no perſon appearing inclined to riſk the enterpriſe, the council broke up.

On the enſuing day Mr. Thomas, of his own accord, took an opportunity, when the enemy were off their guard, to ſtorm the redoubt. Repeated attempts were made by the enemy to regain poſſeſſion, but he bravely maintained himſelf in it, till a reinforcement arriving they gave up the conteſt. Mr. Thomas immediately fortified the poſt.

The parallel was advanced, and the garriſon perceiving no chance of ſuccour from without, the commandant negotiated, and as a ranſom for the fort agreed to pay the ſum of two lacs of rupees. Mr. Thomas received a ſum ſufficient to reimburſe him for the expences he had incurred, and was then directed to return to his own diſtricts. Soon after his arrival he reſtored them to order.

Mr. Thomas had by this time formed his men into a regiment conſiſting of two battalions; of theſe, one he detached to collect the revenues of the country, and with the other remained at Jyjur.

During theſe tranſactions begum Sumroo, in whoſe ſervice Mr. Thomas had formerly been employed, was now trying every means in her power to effect his ruin. She had even gone ſo far as to bribe the Mahratta officers to adviſe his diſmiſſion; and a body of Mahrattas having joined her army, ſhe marched from Sirdhanna, her capital, and encamped about ſeventeen coſs ſouth-eaſt of Jyjur.

This conduct in the begum Mr. Thomas attributed to the influence of the officers in her ſervice; and more particularly to that of Levaſſo, who not only commanded her troops, but had lately received her hand in marriage.

On every occaſion, he was the declared and inveterate enemy of Mr. Thomas; and had by his influence wrought in the begum her preſent determination.

In the begum's army it was publicly aſſerted, that their preſent deſtination was againſt Mr. Thomas. Her force, conſiſting of four battalions of infantry, twenty pieces of artillery, and about four hundred cavalry, was commanded by officers of tried and acknowledged abilities. Mr. Thomas, having recalled the battalion that had been detached, had now a regiment conſiſting of two thouſand men, ten pieces of artillery, five hundred irregulars, and two hundred cavalry.

The diſſenſions, however, that aroſe among the begum's officers, not only induced her to relinquiſh her intention of attacking Mr. Thomas, but ended in her impriſonment, and the total ſubverſion of her authority. The cauſe of theſe diſſenſions muſt now be traced to its ſource.

Levaſſo, who had the chief command of the

begum's army, was jealous of the authority of Legois. This man is a German; and ſo named from Liege, the place of his nativity. He had been many years in habits of intimacy and friendſhip with Mr. Thomas; and, on the preſent occaſion, had ſtrenuouſly diſſuaded the begum from the propoſed hoſtilities. This conduct having given umbrage to Levaſſo, he by his influence with the begum, procured Legois's degradation; and to render his diſgrace the more mortifying, his place was given to a junior officer.

A conduct ſo inconſiſtent and unjuſt diſguſted the ſoldiers, who for many years had been commanded by Legois, with whom alſo they had often fought and conquered. They remonſtrated, but in vain, againſt the meaſure; finding there was no hope of altering the begum's reſolution, they ſuddenly broke out into open mutiny. They invited Zuffur Yab Khawn, the ſon of the late Sumroo by a former wife, who then reſided at Delhi, to become their commander. In return, they promiſed to ſeat him on the muſnud. For this purpoſe, a deputation of the army, in ſpite of all the exertions of the begum, repaired to Delhi, and ſolemnly tendered him the command. Zuffur Yab Khawn, fearful of the intrigues of his mother-in-law, at laſt conſented. To relieve his apprehenſion, the deputation, in the name of the army, took an oath of fidelity to him on the ſpot.

On the firſt intelligence of the conſpiracy the begum and Levaſſo, with a few of their old ſervants, prepared for flight. It was their intention to have proceeded directly to the Ganges, and to ſeek refuge in the country of the vizier Aſuph ool Dowla.

In this reſolution, however, they were unfortunately intercepted. A party of cavalry which had been detached by Zuffur Yub Khawn on the firſt intimation of their flight, overtook and ſurrounded them at the village of Kerwah, in the begum's jaghire, four miles diſtant from her capital. Previous to the commencement of hoſtilities the commandant of cavalry proclaimed a free pardon, and promiſe of their arrears, to the ſoldiers who ſtill adhered to the begum, on condition of their laying down their arms, and delivering up the begum and her huſband.

In the confuſion that aroſe, and before any reſolution could be taken, ſome ſhot were fired, and a few men ſlightly wounded. The ſoldiers, perceiving they had nothing to hope from the begum (who, they knew, only wiſhed to get away with her effects), openly declared themſelves for Sumroo's ſon. The infantry then ſurrounding her palanquin demanded her to ſurrender; the cavalry at the ſame time ſurrounded her huſband, who was on horſeback. The begum at that inſtant drew a poniard from her ſide, and running the point of it acroſs her breaſt drew a little blood, but with no intention of killing herſelf. Her attendants calling for aſſiſtance, Levaſſo hearing the tumult demanded to know what had happened. He was anſwered that the begum had killed herſelf: twice he put the ſame queſtion, and receiving the ſame anſwer, with great deliberation he put a piſtol to his mouth, ſhot himſelf, and immediately fell from his horſe. "The villains (ſays Mr. Thomas) who, the preceding

" day, had ſtyled themſelves his ſlaves, now " committed every act of inſult and indignity " upon his corpſe!" For three days it lay expoſed to the inſults of the rabble, and was at length thrown into a ditch.

Meanwhile Zuffur Yub Khawn advanced to Sirdhanna, whither the begum had already been conducted a priſoner; and having aſſumed the government of the jaghire, tranquillity was ſoon re-eſtabliſhed.

Freed from the apprehenſion of hoſtilities, Mr. Thomas now ſeduloully employed himſelf in the arrangement of the diſtricts.

Appakandarow, who during the late events had found means to ſow diſſenſions between Luckwa and Bappoo Fernevefe, now reaped the fruits of his addreſs. Finding theſe commanders at variance, he prepared to return to Kanond; and while on the march to that place, ſent written orders to Mr. Thomas to diſmiſs the collectors who had been appointed by Bappoo, and to reinſtate his own.

Mr. Thomas obeyed; but Bappoo's army amounting to three thouſand men, it coſt the lives of many to diſpoſſeſs him.

This affair however being at length terminated, Mr. Thomas had the long-expected interview with Appa. They met at Narnoul, a place which had that morning ſurrendered to his arms. After the ſtrongeſt expreſſions of ſatisfaction, and of the ſenſe he entertained of his ſervices, as proof of thoſe ſentiments Appakandarow preſented Mr. Thomas with an elephant, a palanquin, ſhawls, and other articles of value.

A reception ſo cordial was highly gratifying; but its effect was ſoon diminiſhed when, three days after, Appa demanded the delivery of a Bramin in the ſervice of Bappoo Ferneveſe, from whom he intended to exact a fine.

It muſt here be remarked, that previous to the ſurrender of the fort this man, coming privately to Mr. Thomas's camp, had offered terms for the delivery of the fort, for himſelf and two others who accompanied him; as the reward of his treachery, he required ſecurity of life and property, towhich Mr. Thomas yielded a ready aſſent.

Notwithſtanding theſe aſſurances, Appa, at this time in want of a ſupply of money, inſiſted on his delivery, which Mr. Thomas for the reaſons above ſtated as poſitively declined.

To convince Appa of the juſtneſs of his reaſoning, Mr. Thomas exhibited to that chief his own written orders, which had been communicated at the commencement of hoſtilities. Theſe poſitively ſpecified that the ſervants of Bappoo or his adherents who ſubmitted ſhould not ſuffer either in perſon or fortune, but on the contrary were to be allowed a ſafe conduct and ſuitable eſcort to Mattra or Delhi.

In vain Mr. Thomas ſhewed this order; Appa continued inflexible, and contended moreover that as theſe people had formerly been in his own employ, he had on the preſent occaſion a right to extort money. On quitting the durbar the bramin informed Mr. Thomas that he with others was willing to ſettle accounts with Appa, and only required that perſons of integrity ſhould be appointed to inſpect them. To this likewiſe Appa refuſed his conſent; adding that if Mr. Thomas ſtill heſitated to deliver up the people his own conſequence would thereby be leſſened in the eyes of his army. They parted mutually diſſatisfied with each other. To bring this buſineſs to an iſſue Mr. Thomas ſent a meſſage, offering to procure a perſon who, if the bramin was liberated, ſhould become reſponſible for the adjuſtment of the accounts. Appa, highly enraged, and well knowing that the bramin owed him nothing, not only rejected this propoſal, but declined all further intercourſe.

A few days after this altercation, Appa ſent a meſſage to Mr. Thomas deſiring his attendance in the town. He went thither. On his arrival at the houſe he was informed by the ſervants that Appa was unable to come down. Mr. Thomas, unwilling to give any cauſe for offence, ordered the ſoldiers who had accompanied him to remain below; and aſcending by himſelf, was, by a perſon on whoſe attachment he could rely, introduced into his apartment: to his no ſmall ſurpriſe, that chief appeared in perfect health, but of this Mr. Thomas took no notice. The diſcourſe concerning the Bramin was renewed; and ſhortly after Appa riſing from his ſeat, told Mr. Thomas he intended taking a ſlight repaſt, and would then return. Scarcely had he quitted the room in which they ſat before Mr. Thomas was ſurpriſed by the appearance of ſeveral armed men. He now began to ſuſpect ſome treacherous attempt againſt his perſon might be intended; but with that preſence of mind which on trying occaſions never forſook him, he continued firm on his ſeat, convinced that if on this occaſion he had retired it would have afforded matter of triumph to his enemies.

In this ſituation he remained until Appa returned to an adjoining room; from thence he ſent Mr. Thomas a written order immediately to deliver up the perſons in queſtion. Mr. Thomas perceiving matters were advancing to a criſis, and preferring death to diſhonour, roſe from his ſeat, and reſolutely told the perſon who had delivered the order that he would never perform what was now required; without further discussion he entered the apartment of Appa, his sword being in his hand, but as yet undrawn: the Mahratta chief, on Mr. Thomas's approach, appeared hesitating, and as if he was uncertain how to act; Mr. Thomas perceiving his confusion took this opportunity of paying him the customary compliment, and retiring unmolested, though fully determined to visit him no more.

On his arrival in the camp, Mr. Thomas dispatched his Dewan to Appakandarow with the following message:—"That compelled by "a just indignation against the treachery of his "proceeding, he would no longer serve him." In making this declaration, Mr. Thomas had the satisfaction to find he was supported by the troops; who, fired at the insult offered to a man whom they so highly respected, had declared with unanimous consent that they would remain no longer in the service of Appakandarow. Intimidated by this spirited resolution, Appa now wished to compromise the matter: he sent excuses to Mr. Thomas in mitigation of his treachery, and to ensure confidence came the next day in person to the camp. Willing to ſorget the paſt, Mr. Thomas received his chief with reſpect; and matters having once more been placed on an amicable footing, Appa told Mr. Thomas that he had received letters from Bappoo Farneveſe, requeſting the delivery of the perſons who had occaſioned the differences, as a perſonal favour to himſelf. They were accordingly ſent off to Muttra in the manner propoſed.

Mr. Thomas was now directed to repair to the Mewatty country, to collect the tribute that had become due. Taking leave of Appa, he in a few days arrived at Mewat; his preſence at this juncture was the more neceſſary, perpetual quarrels having ariſen between the collectors of Appakandarow and thoſe who had been recently nominated by the Mahratta commanders. Mr. Thomas, however, by his active and ſpirited conduct on this occaſion, by puniſhing ſome and conciliating others, at laſt brought matters into a favourable train of ſettlement. In the courſe of theſe tranſactions he had been under the neceſſity of taking one of the forts by ſtorm, in which were found ſeveral pieces of artillery, and an abundant ſupply of bullocks and other carriage-cattle. Appakandarow, hearing of this capture, claimed as his right the artillery that had been found in the fort. Mr. Thomas as ſtrenuouſly inſiſted on its being the property of the captors. Repeated altercations enſued, till at length Appakandarow having ſecretly gained over a body of Ghoſſeins, who were proceeding to their annual pilgrimage at Hurdwar, inſtigated them to the attack of Mr. Thomas's camp.

CHAPTER III.

Descriptive account of the Hurdwar, and of the annual pilgrimage—Mr. Thomas defeats the Ghosseins—the districts of Panniput and Sonepput are added to Mr. Thomas's possessions—account of the city of Panniput, and of the canal of Ali Merdan Khan.

THE mountains through which the Ganges flows at Hurdwar, present the spectator with the view of a grand natural amphitheatre; their appearance is rugged, and destitute of verdure; they run in ridges and blunt points, in a direction east and west; at the back of the largest range, rise, towering to the clouds, the lofty mountains of Himmalayah, whose tops are covered with perpetual snow, which on clear days present a most sublime prospect. The large jagged masses, broken into a variety of irregular shapes, added to their stupendous height, impress the mind with an idea of antiquity and grandeur coeval with the creation, and the eternal froſt with which they are encruſted appears to preclude the poſſibility of mortals ever attaining their ſummit.

In viewing this grand ſpectacle of nature, the traveller may eaſily yield his aſſent to, and pardon, the ſuperſtitious veneration of the Hindoo votary who, in the fervour of his imagination, aſſigns the ſummit of theſe icy regions as the abode of the great Mahadeo, or Firſt Cauſe; where, ſeated on his throne of ice, he is ſuppoſed to receive the homage of the ſurrounding univerſe.

Hurdwar is a place of great ſanctity, and rendered memorable for the pilgrimages made thither from a remote antiquity.

About the latter end of March, and beginning of April, the pilgrims from Punjab, Guzurat, and the loweſt points of Bengal, aſſemble in prodigious numbers.

In 1794, not leſs than an hundred and fifty thouſand perſons were aſſembled, though fourteen days were ſtill remaining before the pilgrimage would be completed.

Brima and Biſhun, or the creating and preſerving powers, are the principal objects of worſhip at Hurdwar. The temple, ſituate at the foot of the mountain, is called Brimhakood, or the reſervoir of Brimha. Hither the pilgrims reſort, and after purifying themſelves in the Ganges, they cut off their hair and ſhave themſelves. Thoſe who die during the pilgrimage, are burnt on the banks of the Ganges, and their aſhes thrown into the river.

The pilgrimage to Hurdwar is eſteemed of ſuch conſequence, as to be equivalent to that of Caſi (Benares), Puraug (Allahabad), or Chillumbrum, in the Carnatic; and a devotee who has viſited this place may be excuſed from going to any other the remainder of his days. This pilgrimage never fails to benefit the inhabitants of Hurdwar and the neighbouring villages; as out of the great number who reſort there at the annual period, all perſons are obliged to pay a duſtoor, or tax, to the bramins and chokeydars of the villages. This amounts to a large ſum.

Excluſive of the profits before ſtated, the Mahrattas receive a tax upon horſes and camels coming to the fair; the former paying eight annas per head, and the latter ſix annas; one half of this impoſt is levied at the village Joalahpore, and the remainder at the Hurdwar. Hackerys, or wheel-carriages, pay a tax of eight annas, and the covered doolies for the women two annas. There is likewiſe a reſoom (cuſtom) upon the ſale of horſes and camels, on the former ten per cent. and the latter eight, which is paid equally between the vendor and purchaſer. Another mode by which the inhabitants enrich themſelves is, by raiſing the price of grain and articles of proviſion, though upon the balance this is not much againſt the viſitors; who, bringing along with them the production of their reſpective countries, diſpoſe of their goods to advantage at Hurdwar.

Hence this pilgrimage has been converted into a great fair, where all ſorts of merchandize from various parts of Hindostan are sold.

To Hurdwar are brought horses, camels, mules, cloths from the Punjab, shawls, fruit, saffron, musk, Cashmerian wool, brass, and tutinague; *cherruss*, an intoxicating drug, which bears an excessive price in Bengal; fire-arms from Lahore, and excellent Persian scimitars. These several articles are bought, exchanged, and sold; and, from the assemblage of people composed of so many different nations, the place resembles a grand commercial emporium: added to this, those rajahs and petty chiefs, who visit Hurdwar from religious motives, being attended by their troops, and their respective suites, contribute to accumulate the general mass, so that all is hurry, bustle, noise, and confusion.

But to return to our narrative after this digression. The Mahratta chief afore-mentioned, having instigated the Ghosseins to attack Mr. Thomas in his camp, to encourage them, offered as a reward for their services, the sum of ten thousand rupees. These particulars were communicated to Mr. Thomas by his own vakeel, then reſident with Appa. Incenſed at the indignity offered him by a conduct ſo treacherous, he marched againſt the Ghoſſeins, whom he attacked and defeated with great loſs to them, and to himſelf but trifling. After the encounter, they fled towards Delhi; and not thinking themſelves ſafe there, continued to retreat until they had croſſed the Jumna.

On the retreat of the Ghoſſeins, Mr. Thomas expoſtulated with Appa on the treachery of his conduct. He told him that the late tranſaction was ſo ſhameful, that he could no longer remain in his ſervice. Mr. Thomas particularly expatiated on the treatment ſuſtained by a Mr. Taylor: whom, after unjuſtly depriving of his command, Appa had confined in the fort of Goalier, under the pretext of extorting money; till finding the man was not either to be daunted by threats, or cajoled by promiſes, he had at length given him his liberty. "Such," ſaid Mr. Thomas with indignation, "has been the fate of all who have ſerved "you with fidelity."

As a Mahratta is ſeldom at a loſs for an excuſe, Appa, in anſwer to theſe charges, replied, that his own inability to attend to buſineſs (being confined by illneſs) had occaſioned thoſe who had undertaken to manage his concerns, to act in a manner ſo unworthy; that a dangerous diſorder with which he had been long afflicted was growing worſe every day, and that he wiſhed much for a perſonal interview with Mr. Thomas before his death. In this letter, Appakandarow further urged, that the perſon whom he intended for his ſucceſſor being young and inexperienced, he wiſhed to avail himſelf of the benefit of Mr. Thomas's counſel, Appakandarow being from experience well convinced no other perſon would be equally intereſted with the welfare of his family. Finally he aſſured Mr. Thomas, that in the propoſed interview he would not only clear himſelf from the aſperſions of treachery, but arrange every thing to their mutual ſatisfaction and advantage.

This intimation excited no ſmall degree of ſurpriſe in Mr. Thomas, but from paſt experience he did not chuſe to place implicit reliance in the declaration of the Mahratta chief. He was thus reduced to a critical ſituation: for as on the one hand it was difficult to refuſe the requeſt of ſo powerful a chief; ſo on the other, a laudable regard for his perſonal ſafety, if treachery were intended, induced him to decline the propoſed viſit. From this ſtate of uncertainty and ſuſpenſe he was happily relieved, by intelligence of a numerous body of ſeiks having made an irruption into the Dooab, and were at that time committing depredations in the vicinity of Seharunpore, the capital of the late Gholaum Cadir Khan.

The apprehenſion of all parties was conſiderably augmented, when it was known that on their firſt onſet they had cut to pieces ſome battalions of Mahratta troops ſtationed for the defence of that province.

Although Appakandarow had no particular connexion with Seharunpore, he thought that, in common with other powers, he ought to exert himſelf to prevent further incurſions, eſpecially as his own diſtrict would in all probility be the next invaded by theſe deſperate marauders. He therefore directed Mr. Thomas to march with his whole force, and with all possible expedition, giving the most express injunctions to fight the seiks wherever he might come up with them in the Mahratta territories.

Agreeably to these instructions, Mr. Thomas lost no time in repairing to Jyjut; from whence, crossing the Jumna to the northward of Delhi, he advanced rapidly towards the enemy. They not being inclined for the contest thought proper to retreat, crossed the river, and returned unmolested to the Punjab. Mr. Thomas in this place remarks, that whilst in the service of Begum Sumroo he had encountered the seiks on more than one occasion, and had already given them samples of his method of fighting; and though their number at this time was not more than five thousand men, they had not only defeated the Mahrattas, but compelled them to take shelter in the fort of Jelalabad.

Luckwa, commander of the Mahratta forces, hearing of the disgrace sustained by his troops at Seharunpore, as likewise of the subsequent flight of the feiks on Mr. Thomas's approach, now requeſted of Appa to permit this enterpriſing man to raiſe a body of two thouſand men for the protection of the province of Seharunpore, and other parts of the Mahratta poſſeſſions. To this requeſt Appa, though with difficulty, complied; and in conſequence of the purgunahs of Panniput, Sonepat, and Karnaul, were aſſigned to Mr. Thomas, for the payment of two thouſand infantry, two hundred cavalry, and ſixteen pieces of field artillery. Bappoo Scindiah was nominated to the government of Seharunpore; which with the country adjacent, at the period we are ſpeaking of, yielded an annual revenue of ten lacks of rupees.

The ſituation of the city of Panniput, and the celebrated canal in its neighbourhood, may perhaps juſtify a digreſſion in its favour, and curioſity will be gratified in the detail of its ancient and preſent ſtate.

Panniput is a city of great antiquity, and was inhabited by Mahomedans in the reign of Mahmoud of Ghuzna; who, during one of his incurſions into Hindooſtan, ſettled a colony at that place. In the time of the emperor Shah Jehan, it was a populous city; and in the reign of Mahomed Shah, was ſelected by that prince as his principal reſidence. In the year 900 of the Hijira, or A. D. 1525, the Mogul emperor Mahomed Baber invaded Hindooſtan: Ibrahim Lodi of the Patan dynaſty at that time ſat on the throne of Delhi.

He prepared to reſiſt the invader; and aſſembling his forces, conducted them towards the frontiers. The rival armies met on the plains of Panniput; and a general engagement enſued, in which the forces of Ibrahim were totally defeated, and himſelf ſlain. The deceaſed monarch was interred on the ſpot where he fell, by the command of Baber, who directed a tomb to be erected to his memory. This tomb is ſtill to be ſeen, about three miles to the north-weſt of the city. In commemoration of the victory, the Mogul prince directed a magnificent moſque to be built on the ſpot where his own tent was pitched, on the eaſtern ſide of the city. It is called Cabil Baug.

This building, which exhibits one of the firſt ſpecimens of Mahomedan grandeur among the Mogul race of princes, conſiſts of a ſpacious apartment of forty feet ſquare, with others adjoining. It is ſurmounted at top by a magnificent dome, with ſix-and-twenty others of ſmaller dimenſions. Theſe are attached to different apartments on each ſide of the moſque. To the eye this building has a very grand effect, but it is difficult to deſcribe. The edifice is ſurrounded by a high wall of conſiderable length, and within the encloſure are convenient habitations for the attendants on the moſque. The wall is flanked with octangular pavilions of red ſtone, and the entrances through the gateways are of the ſame materials.

The plain of Panniput has likewiſe been celebrated in the hiſtory of modern times. It was on this plain that the famous battle was fought in 1762 between Ahamed Shah, the Duranny, and the Mahrattas. The latter were commanded by Viſwas Raou, a prince of the Mahratta empire, who was ſlain in the conteſt. The loſs of this action wreſted from the Mahrattas the sovereignty of Hindoostan; though the supineness and effeminacy of Ahamed Shah, after his success, prevented his enjoying the fruits of his victory.*

The city of Panniput is situated in 29° 22′ of north latitude. Its circumference may be about four miles. It was formerly surrounded by a brick wall, which in many places is still entire. This wall, and a noble caravansera of stone adjoining the Delhi gate, was built at the expence of Nuwaub Roshun Al Dowlah, grand-chamberlain of the household to Mahomed Shah. The remains of the Delhi gate are still handsome. It is built of brick, forty feet in height, arched at the top and flanked with towers of red stone, and is connected by

* The particulars of this battle have been too ably detailed by the pen of colonel Brown, in a letter to the Asiatic Society, to require comments in this place. It is here sufficient to remark, that no remains of the entrenched camp of the Mahrattas are now to be seen, the plain being perfectly level. But about a mile east of the city, two trees were pointed out to us by the natives, as the place where the Bhow's tent was pitched previous to the battle.

a rampart within the city wall. The exterior of this gateway is encrusted with very fine chunam, and decorated with paintings of flowers, in various patterns, executed in a style of peculiar neatness and delicacy.

In the centre of the city is the shrine of a Mahommedan devotee, by name Shah Shurfuddeen Boo Ali Culinder, the son of Furruckuddeen Iraki. Since his death, which happened in the 724th year of the Hijerah, this mausoleum has been repaired several times. The tomb is situated at the upper end of a spacious square, at the entrance to which is a screen of perforated stone-work; beyond this is the verandah or portico, the roof of which is supported by four pillars of *sungmuhuk*, a species of black marble; the pillars are twelve feet in height, having pedestals of porphyry. The cieling of this portico is decorated with paintings of flowers on fine chunam; along the front of the vestibule, on a slab of white marble, are engraved couplets in the Persian language in black marble characters. These verses are in praise of the sanctity of the deceased, and by the operation of the arithmetical verſe called ABJUD,* give the date of his death in the 724th year of the Hijerah.

Within the dome is the grave of Boo Ali Culinder: it is ſix feet by three, of white marble, and is covered by a pall of rich brocade. The whole is ſurrounded by a latticework of wood. Above is a covering of green ſilk, ſupported by four pillars of wood, encruſted with mother of pearl.

The revenues of this tomb were formerly conſiderable; but moſt of them, during the troubles which have ſubſiſted in the upper provinces, have long ſince been confiſcated.

* The arithmetical verse called ABJUD, consists of the letters of the Arabic alphabet joined together so as to form articulate sounds, but without any meaning. It may be given as follows in *Roman character:*

Abjud, Huwwuz, huttee, Cullamun; Saufuz, kurshut sukkhuz, Zuzzug.

Each of these letters having a numerical property, from one to one thousand, by this operation the dates of inscriptions are discovered. See Richardson's Dictionary, article *Abjud.*

However, ſtill there are from four to five hundred perſons attendant on the ſhrine. Theſe ſubſiſt on the contributions of the charitable.

The city, though now much decayed, and the population reduced, formerly contained many good houſes. The bazars, of which there are two, are of conſiderable length, but narrow; they contain about three hundred ſhops tolerably well furniſhed. The trade of this place conſiſts in imports of ſalt, grain of all kinds, and cotton cloths: they export coarſe ſugar.

In the flouriſhing times of the empire, Panniput, ſituated in the high road to Lahore, Cabul, and Perſia, was the emporium of the caravans from the north, and the ſeat of an extenſive commerce. But the ravages occaſioned by the diſtracted ſtate of the empire, for more than half a century, have not only cauſed a ſad reverſe, but almoſt annihilated its commercial relations with other countries.

CANAL OF ALI MERDAN KHAN.

In the reign of Shah Jehan, Ali Merdan Khan, a nobleman of the court of Perſia, who had revolted from Shah Abaſs, entered into the ſervice of the Mogul prince, having previouſly delivered up the important fortreſs of Candahar, of which he was governor.

This nobleman, being a man of a public ſpirit and a pattern of munificence, dug at his own expence a canal from the vicinity of the city of Panniput, near the head of the Dooab, which extended to the ſuburbs of Delhi. It comprehended a tract of ninety miles in the extent, by which means the villages in the neighbourhood, and every where within its influence, received a moſt ſurpriſing benefit in the cultivation of their lands.

This noble canal* runs in a direction from north to ſouth, and is in general about ten miles diſtant from the Jumna, until it joins

* It is called by the natives NEHUR BEHEISHT, or "*canal of paradise.*"

that river nine miles below the city of New Delhi. From this canal, while it exiſted, a revenue was produced to the royal treaſury of fourteen lacks of rupees per annum. At preſent it is out of repair, dried up, and in many places almoſt deſtroyed; and in the hands of the Mahrattas, its preſent poſſeſſors, the cultivation of the adjacent country ſcarcely yields a lack of rupees.

CHAPTER IV.

Reſtoration to her authority of the Begum Somroo—account of Sirdhannah—death and character of Appakandarow—capture of Samli—Mr. Thomas marches to Panniput.

RESUMING our narrative after the foregoing digreſſion, it is neceſſary to remark that about this time Begum Somroo, whoſe depoſition from authority we have before noticed, ſtill remained a priſoner at Sirdhannah. In a manner the moſt abject and deſponding, ſhe addreſſed Mr. Thomas; ſhe ſtated her apprehenſions of being poiſoned, or otherwiſe put to death; affirmed that her only dependance was on him, implored him to come to her aſſiſtance, and, finally, offered to pay any ſum of money the Mahrattas ſhould require, on condition they would reinſtate her in her Jaghire.

On receipt of theſe letters, Mr. Thomas, by

an offer of 120,000 rupees, prevailed on Bappoo Scindia to make a movement towards Sirdhannah. Convinced from his former experience, that unleſs he could gain over a part of the troops under Zaffer Yab Khan to the Begum's intereſt, not only his exertions would be fruitleſs, but that ſhe herſelf would be expoſed to the greateſt perſonal danger, he therefore ſet on foot a negotiation for this purpoſe, in which having ſucceeded, he marched and encamped with his whole force at the village of Kathoolee, eight coſs to the north-eaſt of Sirdhannah. Here Mr. Thomas publicly gave out that unleſs the Begum was reinſtated in her authority, thoſe who reſiſted muſt expect no mercy; and to give additional weight to this declaration, heappriſed them that he was acting under the orders of the Mahratta chiefs.

This intimation was at firſt attended with deſired effect. Part of the troops belonging to the garriſon inſtantly mutinied, confined Zaffer Yab Kkan, and declared for the begum. Mr. Thomas, however, who well knew that no reliance could be placed on the capricious temper of troops accuſtomed to frequent mutinies, loſt no time in advancing to Sirdhannah, but before he reached that place, a counter-revolution had already proclaimed the reſtoration of Sumroo's ſon.

Eſcorted by only fifty horſe of approved fidelity, Mr. Thomas entered the cantonments, having at the time he ſet out directed four hundred of his infantry to follow him with all poſſible expedition; the arrival of the latter force was particularly fortunate, as Zaffer Yab Khan, on Mr. Thomas's firſt appearance, perceiving him ſlightly attended, thought he had now got him into his power, and inſtructed his ſoldiers to threaten him with inſtant death; but at that moment the reinforcement abovementioned arriving, and the mutineers thinking the whole Mahratta force was at hand, not only gave over their deſign, but now became as ſubmiſſive as they had before been inſolent.

Abandoning the cauſe of Somroo's ſon, they endeavoured, through the Begum's mediation, to deprecate the reſentment of the Mahratta commanders: to this the Begum having conſented, an oath of fidelity was adminiſtered to the troops, and ſhe was finally reinſtated in the full authority of her Jaghire.

Somroo's ſon, after being plundered of his effects, was reconducted a priſoner to Delhi. Part of the ſum ſtipulated was now paid to Bappoo Scindia, and the remainder promiſed. An interview took place between the Begum and the Mahratta chiefs, when every thing being amicably adjuſted, the army quitting Sirdhannah repaired to their reſpective deſtinations.

The reſtoration of the Begum to her authority, affords us an opportunity of giving a detailed account of her Jaghire.

Sirdhannah, the reſidence of Begum Somroo, is the capital of a ſmall principality, ſituated in the centre of the Dooab, in latitude 29° 10′ north, and about thirty-five coſſes diſtant from Delhi. This Jaghire was from early times rich and fruitful: it was firſt peopled by a Hindoo rajah named Sirkhut. When the famous Mahmood of Ghuzna invaded Hindooſtan, he ſettled a colony of Muſſulmans in this diſtrict, and diſtributed lands to them in ſeveral parts of the country. When the poſterity of Timoor became firmly ſeated on the throne of India, Sirdhannah was firſt attached to the province of Sehaurunpore, ſituated at the head of the Dooab, and at the foot of the mountains called Sewalick. In the reign of Mahmood Shah it was aſſigned as a Jaghire to the famous Kummur Uddeen Khan; and ſubſequent to that period it was held by an omrah named Yacoob Ali Khan, of the court of Alumgeer the Second.

On the death of that monarch, the province of Sehaurunpore was poſſeſſed by the Nawaub Nujuff Khan, prime miniſter to the preſent king, and he allotted Sirdhannah and its dependancy to Somroo, a German, who had been in the ſervice of Coſſim Ali Khan, the depoſed ſubah of Bengal. This man is well known to the Engliſh by the ſhare he bore in the dreadful cataſtrophe of Patna. On the death of Somroo, which happened in the year 1776, Nujuff Khan delivered over the pergunnah to his widow the preſent Begum, on condition of her keeping up a ſorce of three battalions of infantry for the protection of the province.

When Nujuff Khan died, the Begum ſtill kept poſſeſſion of her jaghire, from which time until the period we are ſpeaking of, her ſituation has been fully detailed in recent publications.*

The habitation of Begum Somroo is in a large and ſpacious incloſure, equal in many reſpects to a fortified town. The houſe is well built, and handſomely furniſhed, partly after the European and partly after the Hindooſtany ſtyle: theſe blended together have a ſingular though not upon the whole an unpleaſing appearance. Hoſpitable in her manner, the Begum's table is furniſhed with every thing the country can afford. European articles of all kinds are procured from Calcutta.

It has been the conſtant and invariable uſage of this lady to exact from her ſubjects and ſervants the moſt rigid attention to the cuſtoms

* Consult the History of Shah Aulum.

of Hindooſtan. She is never ſeen out of doors, or in her public durbar unveiled.

Her officers and others, who have buſineſs with her, preſent themſelves oppoſite the place where ſhe ſits. The front of her apartments is furniſhed with *chicques* or Indian ſcreens, theſe being let down from the roof. In this manner ſhe gives audience, and tranſacts buſineſs of all kinds. She frequently admits to her table the higher ranks of her European officers, but never admits the natives to come within the incloſure. On dinner being announced, twenty or thirty of her female attendants, moſt of them chriſtians, repairing to the outer door, there receive the diſhes and place them upon table; they wait on the company during the repaſt, which is always plentiful and well ſerved.*

* Begum Somroo is about forty-five years of age, small in stature, but inclined to be plump. Her complexion is very fair, her eyes black, large, and animated; her dress perfectly Hindoostany, and of the most costly materials. She speaks the Persian and Hindoostany languages with fluency, and in her conversation is engaging, sensible, and spirited.

The Begum being thus reſtored to her authority, Mr. Thomas next received orders to proceed to Samli, and puniſh the commandant of that place for his conduct in encouraging the ſeiks in their intended incurſions into the Dooab, and having communicated to them the defenceleſs ſtate of the upper provinces.

After a fatiguing and difficult march of thirty coſs in one day, Mr. Thomas arrived before Samli.* An action took place, in which the commandant, after a moſt gallant reſiſtance, was defeated, and compelled to retreat into the town. Mr. Thomas, perceiving the

* Samli is a large town situated near the head of the Dooab, in the province of Sehaurunpore. It is two miles in circumference, and contains many handsome houses both of brick and stone. The streets intersect each other at right angles, and have separate gates at their entrances, which at night are shut for the security of the inhabitants. At Samli is a large bazar and a mint where money used formerly to be coined. But the trade of this place, like many others in the Dooab, is now much on the decline; and, with the exception of a few coarse cloths, the manufactures are at a stand. In its present state, the villages attached to the pergunnah of Samli yield a revenue of about 50,000 rupees, though in the flourishing times of the empire it was far more considerable.

neceſſity of bringing this affair to a ſpeedy concluſion, in the evening of the ſame day gave orders for an aſſault, and carried the place by ſtorm. The commandant, his ſon, and moſt of his adherents, were cut to pieces.

Having arranged the affairs of Samli, and appointed a civil governor on the part of the Mahrattas, Mr. Thomas repaired to the camp of Bappoo Scindia, with whom, by order of Appakandarow, he now acted in concert.

Bappoo Scindia, when joined by Mr. Thomas, was employed in the reduction of Lucnowty, a place of conſiderable ſtrength. A practicable breach being effected, preparations were made for ſtorming; when the commandant, ſeeing he was likely to be unſucceſsful in defending the fort, to ſave a further effuſion of blood, came privately to Mr. Thomas's tent, and there made terms for the delivery of the place, which, on the enſuing morning, were performed with punctuality.

A circumſtance now aroſe which had conſiderable effect not only with regard to the immediate ſituation of Mr. Thomas's affairs, but in changing the future fortune of his eventful life.

Two days previous to the reduction of Samli, he received a letter from Appakandarow, in which that chief informed Mr. Thomas, that from continued illneſs his pains were augmented to a degree which had now become intolerable, and no hopes appearing of recovery from the cruel diſtemper under which he laboured, he had determined to put a period to his miſery by a voluntary death! For this purpoſe he was on his way to the Ganges, but requeſted of Mr. Thomas to come and ſee him once more before the ſcene was cloſed for ever.

On receipt of this intelligence, Mr. Thomas ſet out immediately to meet, and, if poſſible, afford conſolation to his deſponding chief; but he had not advanced far, when the melancholy intelligence reached him of Appakandarow's having voluntarily drowned himſelf in the river Jumna.

Such was the end of Appakandarow, a chief

intrepid and enterprizing, who, amid the tranſactions of later times, and the various revolutions of Mahratta politics in Hindooſtan, had borne an active and diſtinguiſhed part.

The death of Appa was on ſeveral accounts unfavourable to Mr. Thomas's intereſts. Vavon Row, his nephew and ſucceſſor, was a youth vain and inexperienced, and better adapted to the life of an accomptant than that of a general.

Inſtigated by the ſuggeſtions of perſons who ſurrounded him, the incautious youth was perſuaded to demand reſtitution from Mr. Thomas of the diſtricts which had been given him by his uncle, as an honorable reward for the ſervices he had performed. Agreeably to this reſolution, he had the weakneſs to order his troops to take poſſeſſion of the diſtricts in queſtion.

Mr. Thomas, indignant at a conduct he ſo little merited, peremptorily refuſed compliance with the order. He repreſented to that chief, by letter, the impropriety of his preſent proceeding; declared his firm reſolution to maintain poſſeſſion of the diſtricts; pointed out to him the fatal effects that muſt neceſſarily ariſe to both parties if the quarrel was purſued further; and, finally, for the ſake of peace, and to prevent future diſagreements, acquainted Vavan Row that he was willing to pay a ſum of money if left in quiet poſſeſſion.

Theſe remonſtrances, however founded on reaſon or juſtice, were of no avail: Vavon Row would liſten to no terms but the implicit ceſſion of the whole. The matter could therefore only be decided by an appeal to the ſword.

On Mr. Thomas's arrival at Hoſſellee, a large village forming part of his poſſeſſions, he perceived it in the hands of the enemy; and Vavon Row, prepared to defend it, encamped under the walls of the fort.

Unwilling to puſh matters to an extremity, if by any means it could be avoided, Mr. Thomas drew off his force to a ſmall diſtance, and gave particular orders to his own people to forbear all acts of hoſtility on their part. This mode of conduct was of no avail; for the troops of Vavon Row coming daily from their own camp, insulted and fired upon Mr. Thomas's men, by which several of them were severely wounded.

The enemy, reinforced by a large body of the peasantry, and headed by the zemindars of their respective villages, were now become so formidable, that Mr. Thomas resolved to bring the business to an issue. He accordingly attacked them. The affair was quickly decided; the enemy fled in all directions; and the greater part, having taken shelter in the fort of Kussollee, were followed by Mr. Thomas, who immediately commenced the siege of that place. Having erected batteries, he ordered the grates for heating shot to be got in readiness; which being done, he fired so successfully with red-hot shot, that he quickly compelled them to surrender at discretion.

It was now agreed that an interview betwixt Mr. Thomas and Vavon Row should take place at Kanond, whither the former had marched for that purpose. On his arrival, however, Vavon Row, pretending to be fearful of treachery, refufed to come out of the fort; and Mr. Thomas, for fimilar reafons, was unwilling to enter it. The negotiations were therefore broken off; and Mr. Thomas, continuing to confider this Mahratta chief as an enemy, led his troops toward the frontiers.

This meafure was rendered more neceffary, and his attention called to the defence of his northern purgunnahs, which had recently been invaded by the feiks.

But the mention of this remarkable people, leading us afide for a while from the ordinary courfe of our narrative, invites a detail of the prefent ftate of the Punjaub, or country fituated between the Indus and the Sutledge.

CHAPTER V.

Geographical deſcription of the Punjab,—of the ſeiks, their manners, cuſtoms, forces, and reſources.

THE extenſive and fertile country deſcribed by Arrian and other antient hiſtorians, as comprehended within the five great rivers, the Hydaſpes, the Hydraötes, the Aceſines, the Hyphaſis, and the Sutledge, is, by modern geographers, denominated Punjab.

On the north it is bounded by the mountains inhabited by the tribe called Yooſuf Zey; on the eaſt by the mountains of Naun, Serinnaghur and Jumbo; on the weſt by the river Sind or Attock;* and on the ſouth by the diſtricts of Panniput, and the province of Harrianah. It is two hundred and fifty coſſes from

* This river above the city of Attock is called by the natives Aba Seen.

north to ſouth, and nearly one hundred from eaſt to weſt. Notwithſtanding the ſtate of warfare in which the chiefs of Punjab are conſtantly involved, the country is in a ſtate of high cultivation; and though the population be great, grain is cheaper than in any other part of India. This advantage in a great meaſure is derived from the numerous rivers by which it is watered. Advancing from the ſouth, a traveller meets in rapid ſucceſſion the Serſooty, the Cugger, the Chowah, and the Sutledge.

The Serſooty, after paſſing the towns of Mooſtufabad, Shahabad, and Tehnaſſer, and overflowing the country on each of its banks, joins itſelf to the Cugger to the north-weſt of Kaythul.

The Cugger, on the contrary, after paſſing the towns of Bunnoor, Seyfabad, Puttialah, Jowhana, and Jomalpore, enters the country of the Batties at the town of Arwah, formerly the capital of the diſtrict. The Chowah, in like manner, after paſſing through an extenſive tract of country which it fertilizes and enriches, is finally loſt in the ſands of Sonáum.

The Punjab yields to no part of India in fertility of ſoil ; it produces in the greateſt abundance, ſugar-cane, wheat, barley, rice, pulſe of all ſorts, tobacco, and various fruits ; and it is alſo well ſupplied with cattle. The principal manufactures of this country are ſwords, match-locks, cotton cloths, and ſilks both coarſe and fine.

This nation, if united, could bring into the field from fifty to ſixty thouſand cavalry, but it is Mr. Thomas's opinion that they will never unite or be ſo formidable to their neighbours as they have heretofore been. Internal commotions and civil ſtrife have of late years generated a ſpirit of revenge and diſunion among the chiefs, which it will take a long time to overcome.

The number of cavalry which it is ſuppoſed this nation was able to aſſemble has been conſiderably over-rated, in conſequence of a cuſtom which formerly obtained among the Sciks, of forming an aſſociation of their forces under a particular chief. From this aſſociation of their forces they had the general intereſts of the community in view. To thoſe who were ignorant of the ſecret cauſes of the aſſociation, this junction of forces was frequently miſtaken for the army of an individual; and this error was perhaps increaſed by the natural partiality of the Seiks themſelves to magnify the force and enhance the character of their own nation.

It has been remarked, that the Seiks are able to collect from fifty to ſixty thouſand horſe; but, to render this number effective, thoſe who do not take the field, or who remain at home to guard their poſſeſſions, muſt be included.

Eſtimating the force of the different diſtricts, the aggregate will be ſeen in the ſubjoined ſchedule.*

	Cavalry.
* The diſtricts south of the Sutledge, -	15,000
The Dooab, or country between the Sutledge and Beyah, - - -	8,000
Between the Beyah and Rowee, - -	11,000
Force of Bugheel Sing, chief of Pattialah, -	12,000
The countries above Lahore, the inhabitants of which are chiefly under the influence of Runjeet Sing, - - -	11,000
To which may be added the force of Nizamud-deen Khan, - - -	5,000
Roy Elias, - - -	1,300
Other Patan chiefs, in pay of the Seiks, -	800
Grand total -	64,000

By this ſtatement it will appear that the entire force of this nation, excluſive of the diſtrict held by Zemaun Shah, eaſtward of the Attock,* can amount to no more than ſixty-four thouſand men, and of theſe two-thirds might probably take the field, were a chief of experience and enterprize to appear amongſt them; but this in Mr. Thomas's opinion is highly improbable. The chief of moſt conſequence at preſent is Runjeet Sing: he having poſſeſſion of Lahore, which may be termed the capital of the Punjab, has acquired a decided aſcendancy over the other chiefs, though he be frequently in a ſtate of warfare with his neighbours who inhabit that part of the country ſituated between the Beyah and the Rawee. This chief is deemed by the natives as the moſt powerful among them. He poſſeſſes one thouſand horſe, which are his own property.

The repeated invaſion of the Punjab by ſmall armies, of late years, affords a convincing proof that the national force of the ſeiks cannot be

* These diſtricts are computed to reach from Sirhind to the banks of that river.

ſo formidable as has been repreſented. Several inſtances occur in ſupport of this aſſertion. Not many years ſince, Dara Row Scindia invaded it at the head of ten thouſand men; though not more than ſix thouſand of that number deſerved the name of troops, the remainder being a deſpicable rabble. Though joined on his march by two chiefs, Buggeel Sing and Kurrum Sing, he was at length oppoſed by Sahib Sing, the chief of Fyzealpore. That chief was encamped under the walls of Kuſſoor,* having the river Cugger in his front; was defeated in an engagement, and the enſuing day the fort ſurrendered. Sahib Sing then agreed to pay the Mahrattas a ſum of money, and moſt of the chiefs ſouth of the Sutledge having by this time ſubmitted to Dara Row, oppoſition was at an end.

It was ſucceſſively invaded by the armies of Ambajee, Bala Row, and Nana Furkiah, who drove the ſeiks repeatedly before them.

In 1800 Mr. Thomas himſelf entered their country at the head of five thouſand troops and

* Kussoor, a fort south of the river Sutledge.

ſixty pieces of artillery; and though by the inſtigation of enemies, who promiſed them aſſiſtance, the chiefs ſouth of the Sutledge and in the Dooab (or country between the two rivers*) combined againſt him, yet he penetrated as far as the Sutledge. During that campaign he never ſaw more than ten thouſand Seiks in one army: he remained in their country ſix months, two of which were paſſed without competition, and he finally compelled them to purchaſe peace.

Of late years the rajah of Serinnagur has likewiſe made ſome conqueſts in Punjab, chiefly between the Beyah and the Sutledge; and Nizamuddeen Khan, the patan before mentioned, has alſo acquired territory yielding a revenue of three lacks of rupees per annum.

The Seiks, though united, have never made any conſiderable oppoſition againſt the force of Zemaun Shah, who has frequently attacked them; but it may be urged, that a great difference is to be expected from a formidable

* The Beyah and the Sutledge.

army of ſixty thouſand men, led on by the Shah in perſon, and the princes of the blood, compared with the detached bodies already deſcribed. Hence it would appear that this nation is not ſo formidable as they have been repreſented, and in all probability they never will be formidable when oppoſed by regular troops.

The Seiks are armed with a ſpear, matchlock, and ſcymetar. Their method of fighting, as deſcribed by Mr. Thomas, is ſingular: after performing the requiſite duties of their religion by ablution and prayer, they comb their hair and beards with peculiar care; then mounting their horſes, ride forth towards the enemy, with whom they engage in a continued ſkirmiſh, advancing and retreating until man and horſe become equally fatigued. They then draw off to ſome diſtance from the enemy, and meeting with cultivated ground, they permit their horſes to graze of their own accord, while they parch a little gram for themſelves; and after ſatisfying nature by this frugal repaſt, if the enemy be near, they renew the ſkirmiſhing. Should he have retreated they provide forage for their cattle, and endeavour to procure a meal for themſelves.

Seldom indulging in the comforts of a tent, whilſt in the enemy's country, the repaſt of a ſeik cannot be ſuppoſed to be either ſumptuous or elegant. Seated on the ground with a mat ſpread before them, a bramin, appointed for the purpoſe, ſerves out a portion of food to each individual, the cakes of flour which they eat during the meal ſerving them in the room of diſhes and plates.*

The ſeiks are remarkably fond of the fleſh

* Does not this circumstance recall our ideas to the situation of Æneas and his companions, shortly after their landing on the coast of Italy? The condition of Æneas exhibits a specimen of primeval simplicity of manners among the Romans, no less singular than the coincidence of cuſtoms exiſting in Punjab at the present day appears strikingly intereſting.

Consumtis hic forte aliis, ut vertere morsus
Exiguam in Cererem penuria adegit edendi,
Et violare manu malisq. audacibus orbem
Fatalis cruſti, patulis nec parcere quadris,
Heus! etiam mensas consumimus, inquit Iulus.

Virg. Æn. lib. 7.

of the jungle hog, which they kill in the chace: this food is allowable by their law. They likewise eat of mutton and fish; but these being deemed unlawful the bramins will not partake, leaving those who chuse to transgress their institutes to answer for themselves. In the city or in the field the seiks never smoke tobacco: they are not, however, averse to drinking spirituous liquors, in which they sometimes indulge to an immoderate excess; and they likewise freely take opium, bang, and other intoxicating drugs. In their convivial parties each man is compelled to drink out of his own vessel.

Accustomed from their earliest infancy to a life of hardship and difficulty, the seiks despise the comforts of a tent; in lieu of this, each horseman is furnished with two blankets, one for himself and the other for his horse. These blankets, which are placed beneath the saddle, with a gram bag and heel ropes, comprize, in time of war, the baggage of a seik. Their cooking utensils are carried on tattoos. Considering this mode of life, and the extraordinary rapidity of their movements, it cannot be matter of wonder if they perform marches, which, to those who are only accustomed to European warfare, must appear almost incredible.

The Seiks, among other customs singular in their nature, never suffer their hair or beards to be cut: consequently, when mounted on horseback, their black flowing locks and half-naked bodies, which are formed in the stoutest and most athletic mould, the glittering of their arms, and the size and speed of their horses, render their appearance imposing and formidable, and superior to most of the cavalry of Hindoostan.

In the use of their arms, especially the matchlock and sabre, they are uncommonly expert; some use bows and arrows. In addition to the articles of dress which have been described in recent publications * of the times, Mr. Thomas mentions that the arms and wrists of the Seiks are decorated with bangles of gold, silver, brass, and iron, according to the circum-

* Consult the History of Shah Aulum.

ſtances of the wearers; but among the chiefs of the reſpective tribes, the horſe-furniture, in which they take the greateſt pride (and which, with the exception of the inlaying of their fire-arms, is their luxury), is uncommonly ſplendid; for, though a ſeik will ſcruple to expend the moſt trifling ſum on his food or clothing, he will ſpare no expence in endeavouring to excel his comrades in the furniture of his horſe, and in the richneſs and brightneſs of his armour; a circumſtance which appears to bear no inconſiderable reſemblance to the cuſtoms of the ancient Spartans.*

Conſiderable ſimilarity in their general cuſtoms may be traced with thoſe of the Jauts. Though theſe in ſome diſtricts apparently vary, the difference is not material; and their permitting an interchange of marriages with the Jauts of the Dooab and Harrianah, amounts almoſt to a concluſive proof of their affinity of origin.

The Seiks allow foreigners of every deſcription to join their ſtandard, to ſit in their com-

* See Cornelius Nepos, and Pauſanias.

pany, and to ſhave their beards; but, excepting in the inſtance of the Jauts, they will not conſent to intermarriages; nor will they eat or drink from the hands of an alien, except he be a bramin, and for this caſt they always profeſs the higheſt veneration.

If, indeed, ſome regulations which are in their nature purely military, and which were introduced by their founder Nanick, be excepted, it will be found that the Seiks are neither more or leſs than Jauts in their primitive ſtate.

Thus far, ſays Mr. Thomas, we have ſeen the fair ſide of the picture; let us now conſider the reverſe.—The Seiks are falſe, ſanguinary, and faithleſs; they are addicted to plunder, and the acquirement of wealth by any means, however nefarious. Inſtances have occurred of a child's arm being raiſed againſt his parent, and of brothers deſtroying each other.

Women amongſt them are held in little eſtimation, and though ill treated by their hufbands, and prohibited from accompanying them in their wars, thefe unhappy females nevertheless attend to their domeftic concerns with a diligence and fedulousnefs deferving of a better fate.

Inftances, indeed, have not unfrequently occurred, in which they have actually taken up arms to defend their habitations from the defultory attacks of the enemy, and throughout the conteft behaved themfelves with an intrepidity of fpirit highly praifeworthy.

In the feik army, the modes of payment are various: but the moft common is at the time of harveft, when every foldier receives the amount of his pay in grain and other articles, the produce of the country; to fome is given money in fmall fums, and to others lands are allotted for their maintenance. Three-fifths of the horfes of the Punjab are the property of the different chieftains: the remainder belong to the peafantry who have become fettlers.

A feik foldier has alfo his portion of the plunder acquired in the courfe of a campaign: this is fet afide as a reward for his fervices; and in addition to it, he ſometimes increaſes his gain by ſecreting part of the public plunder.

The nature of the ſeik government is ſingular, and probably had its origin in the unſettled ſtate of the tribe when firſt eſtabliſhed in their poſſeſſions. Within his own domains each chief is lord paramount. He exerts an excluſive authority over his vaſſals, even to the power of life and death; and to increaſe the population of his diſtricts, he proffers a ready and hoſpitable aſylum to fugitives from all parts of India. Hence, in the ſeik territories, though the government be arbitrary, there exiſts much leſs cauſe for oppreſſion than in many of the neighbouring ſtates; and hence likewiſe, the cultivator of the ſoil being liable to frequent change of maſters, by the numerous revolutions that are perpetually occurring, may be conſidered as one of the cauſes of the fluctuation of the national force.*

* In the above sketch of the situation and resources of the seik nation, Mr. Thomas does not include the territories of Zemaun Shah lying east of the Attock; part of which were, during the reigns of the emperors, included in the Punjab, and may therefore be considered as belonging to it.

CHAPTER VI.

Mr. Thomas defeats the Seiks—concludes an advantageous treaty—disagreement with Bappoo Scindia—Mr. Thomas forms the design of establishing himself as an independant chief—for that purpose selects the province of Hurrianah—his establishment at Hansi.

SUCH was the tribe against which Mr. Thomas now prepared to march. Leaving a force competent to the defence of Jyjur, which he expected would be attacked by Vavon Row, he marched to Karnâl, near which the Seiks lay.

Four successive actions took place, attended with considerable loss on both sides; Mr. Thomas having lost five hundred men, and the Seiks double that number. Both parties inclining to peace, a treaty was concluded, by which the Seiks agreed to evacuate the province, which was accordingly done.

As Mr. Thomas had foreseen, he now received intelligence of Vavon Row having laid siege to Jyjur, to defend which he immediately marched back. On his approach, Vavon Row thought proper to retire. Mr. Thomas next determined to punish Cashmiree Bolee, who, as before stated, had been the author and fomenter of all the differences which had occurred betwixt him and Vavon Row. Mr. Thomas, therefore, fell suddenly on the pergunnah of Daderee, which belonged to Cashmiree Bolee, and laid it under contribution.

From hence he was called away to assist Bapoo Scindia against a body of Rohillas, who, instigated by Nevil Sing, a seik chief, had crossed the Ganges, and invaded his possessions near the head of the Dooab. But previous to Mr. Thomas's arrival, the Mahratta chief had not only defeated the invaders, but followed up his blow by laying siege to the enemy's capital.

A body of Seiks had assembled to assist him; but, on the approach of Mr. Thomas's force, thought proper to separate; and Bapoo Scindia, not deeming the capture of this fort worth the trouble it would take to gain poſſeſſion, of his own accord ſoon after raiſed the ſiege, and returned to Seharunpore. Mr. Thomas remained with his force at Soneput, a city twenty-ſix miles ſouth of Panniput, the neighbouring country, barren and deſolate.

North of this city is a mauſóleum erected by Khizzer Khan, a Patan nobleman, deſcended from the royal family of Sheer Shah. This building is an octagon, ſurmounted by a ſpacious dome, and ornamented at the top with a cullis of copper gilt. The interior of the mauſoleum is of grey ſtone, the cornices are embelliſhed with ſculpture ornaments of red freeſtone, and around the lower part of the dome runs a ſtone border, on which are engraved verſes from the Koran in Arabic characters. The front of the building is decorated with roſes cut in freeſtone, of a brown colour; the whole uncommonly delicate, and has been finiſhed with more than uſual attention.

The pergunnah of Soneput compoſes part of the Jaghire of Deſmouk, ſon-in-law of Scindia, and yields an income of ſeventy-five thouſand rupees. But in the reign of the emperor Mahomed Shah, this pergunnah, in conſequence of the benefit it derived from its vicinity to the noble canal of Ali Merdan Khan, is ſaid to have yielded a revenue of nine lacks of rupees.

In the environs of Soneput, a traveller firſt meets with the *coſs minar*, or Indian mile-ſtone. It is a round pillar of brick, ten feet in height, and placed on each ſide of the road, at the diſtance of about three Engliſh miles from each other. They were erected by order of the emperor Jehan Gheer, and formerly extended from Lahor to Agra. Adjoining to each of theſe pillars is a well, lined with brick, near which are ſtone benches expreſsly for the accommodation of travellers.

Mr. Thomas had not long remained at Soneput, when rumours of the arrival of Zemaun Shah, king of Cabul, at Lahore, induced Bappoo to meet and conſult with him on the preſent emergency.

Mr. Thomas accordingly repaired to Bappoo; but his troops having again fallen in arrears, were become clamorous for payment: this conduct giving offence to Bappoo, a misunderstanding took place between him and Mr. Thomas, when the latter in disgust marched away.

He was soon after attacked by Bappoo's force, who, on hearing of the retreat of the shah, had determined on punishing Mr. Thomas for what he termed his late misbehaviour. An action ensued; but the commander of Bappoo's troops being wounded in the conflict, he thought proper to remove to a distance.

An amicable arrangement between the parties would now have taken place, had not the Seiks in Bappoo's army, aware of Mr. Thomas's intention to enter the Punjab, used their utmost exertions to widen the difference. Hostilities being again renewed, an action took place at the passage of the Jumna; and though the country people had by this time joined the Mahrattas, Mr. Thomas, by a spirited attack, compelled them to leave him a free passage.

Straitened for provifions, he proceeded on his route to the north-eaft frontier. In his retreat, he was followed by Bappoo's army; and the troops of Begum Somroo, as alfo thofe of Ragojee, governor of Delhi, had now increafed the number of his enemies.

Over this combined force, however, he proved victorious; and having defeated the enemy in every attempt to interrupt him on his march, he at length reached the neighbourhood of Panniput. Here, on account of his inferiority in force, he was compelled for the prefent not only to relinquifh the frontier towns, but to confine himfelf to Jyjur. Thither he fhortly after arrived. Unable to fatisfy the demands of his troops, Mr. Thomas now determined to levy contributions on the territories of his neighbours. For this purpofe he led his army to Oreecha, a large and populous town belonging to the rajah of Jypore.

As a ranfom for this place, Mr. Thomas demanded of the governor a lack of rupees; which being denied, he ftormed and took poffeffion of the city. The fort, which was feparate, ftill holding out, he was on the point of making a ſecond aſſault, when the killadâr agreed to ranſom both for fifty-two thouſand rupees. During the negotiations the town had unfortunately been ſet on fire; which burnt ſo fiercely, that it was with difficulty extinguiſhed, and not until goods to the amount of ſeveral lacks of rupees had been totally conſumed.

About this time a reconciliation was effected betwixt Mr. Thomas and Vavon Row, when it was agreed to adjuſt all former differences; and Mr. Thomas, to evince the reconciliation was on his part ſincere, brought under obedience to Vavon Row ſeveral refractory zemindars. He now entered the Jypore country the ſecond time; and the Meenas, a thieviſh tribe inhabiting a part of the country on his route, about thirty coſs north of Jypore, having formerly invaded Vavon Row's poſſeſſions, Mr. Thomas attacked them in force, and in a very ſhort time annihilated this neſt of banditti. After theſe tranſactions, Mr. Thomas returned to Jyjur.

At this place, about the middle of the year

1798, he firſt formed the eccentric and arduous deſign of erecting an independant principality for himſelf. The country of Hurrianah, which, from the troubled ſtate of the times, had for many years acknowledged no maſter, but became in turn the prey of each ſucceeding invader, appeared to him as beſt adapted for the execution of his purpoſe.

The ſcarcity of water, however, in this part of India, induced Mr. Thomas to poſtpone his intended expedition until the approach of the rainy ſeaſon. Having reinforced his army, and being well provided with every thing neceſſary to enſure ſucceſs, he commenced his march.

His firſt attack was directed againſt the town and fort of Kanhoree, the inhabitants of which place were notorious for their thieviſh depredations. Advancing with celerity, Mr. Thomas, according to his uſual cuſtom, attempted to carry the place by ſtorm. In this, however, he was not only prevented by the ſpirited conduct of the enemy, but compelled to retreat with the loſs of three hundred of his men.

In conſequence of this ſevere check, it became neceſſary to fortify his camp; and the conſtant and heavy rains which now fell preventing his erecting batteries, he fortified a chain of poſts round the town, and thereby prevented any ſuccour from without.

The garriſon he well knew was ſtraitened for proviſions; and the ſiege, thus converted into a blockade, augmented their diſtreſs. The enemy, by frequent ſallies, endeavoured to interrupt Mr. Thomas's operations. In one of theſe, an attack was made on the redoubt occupied by himſelf. In the confuſion attendant on a buſineſs of this nature, the greater part of his people, being panic-ſtruck, ran away. Mr. Thomas was thus reduced to a ſituation truly critical: five men only remained with him of the infantry, to whom had been allotted the particular charge of his fire-arms, conſiſting of piſtols and blunderbuſſes of a large ſize. With theſe, and the aſſiſtance of a few horſemen, who had likewiſe adhered to him, he maintained the poſt for a conſiderable time againſt every effort of the enemy; and at length, by repeated and well-directed difcharges, compelled them to retreat.

A few days after this occurrence, the weather becoming more favourable, and Mr. Thomas having rallied the fugitives, erected a battery, from which he fired with fuch good effect, as to bring down a confiderable part of the wall; but night intervening before he could prepare for ftorming, the affault was delayed until the enfuing day. It was however rendered unneceffary by the enemy's having evacuated the town during the night.

The beft and braveft men of Hurrianah being in this town, Mr. Thomas reduced the other places with but little refiftance. In a fhort time he gained complete poffeffion of the whole fouth part of the province; but the north-weftern part being occupied by the Batties, the rajah of Pattyalah, and other feik chieftains, it coft him confiderable time and much trouble to eftablifh his authority as far as the river Cauggur.

The fuccefsful termination of this campaign,

affords us an opportunity of presenting a detailed account of the country possessed by Mr. Thomas; with some relative observations on the nature and quality of the soil, and on the general character of its inhabitants.

In the district called Hurrianah, ninety miles to the north-west of Delhi, is the country of Mr. George Thomas. It extends eighty coss from north to south, and the same distance from east to west. To the northward it is bounded by the possessions of Sahig Sing, chief of Puttialah, on the north-west by the Batties, west by the dominions of Beykaneer, and south by Jypore, south-east by the pergunnah of Dadaree, east by the districts adjoining to Delhi, and north-east by the cities of Rhotuck and Panniput. That part of the country more immediately occupied by Mr. Thomas, is in shape nearly oval, and extends from sixteen to twenty-four coss* in different directions. The northern boundary is formed by the river Caggur, beyond which are the seik territories. To the south it is bounded by the town of Behal,

* Consult the map.

east by Mahim, and west by Behadra, containing in all eight hundred villages.

Within this tract of country, as in most parts of Hurrianah, water is scarce, more especially during the hot season. To remedy this inconvenience, the inhabitants have constructed wells of considerable depth, not unfrequently from one hundred and twenty to one hundred and fifty feet.

In addition to this each district has two or three tanks faced with stone. These afford a plentiful supply of water until the approach of the hot winds of the ensuing season, when they are dried up. The number of wells differ according to the industry of the respective inhabitants. At Hissâr, for instance, are three hundred; at Hansi, thirty; at Mahim, one hundred; Tuhana has only six; and some of the smaller towns from two to five. In this country the Cauggur river is of the greatest service to the inhabitants. It is overflowed during the rainy season by the accession of the streams which issue from the mountains; and on the retiring of the waters, leaves, like the waters of the Nile, a rich and greasy earth, which yields an abundant crop of the finest wheat. Other parts of Mr. Thomas's possessions produce joar, rice, bajerah, and various sorts of pulse, chunah, and barley; but the latter depends on the rain that may fall from the month of October to Christmas. Within the aforementioned tract, the pasturage is uncommonly luxuriant, and produces perhaps the largest supply of forage to be met with in any part of Asia. The grass in Hurrianah is also of a very superior quality, both as to wholesomeness and nourishment. Hence the cattle excel those of other parts. The climate is in general salubrious; though, when the sandy and desert country lying to the westward becomes heated, it is inimical to an European constitution.

The *peyook*, or Guinea-worm, so common in several parts of Arabia and Persia, is likewise extremely troublesome in this province. To some it proves dangerous; though it is remarked by Mr. Thomas, this disorder seldom attacks Europeans, and is in general confined to the peasantry of the country.

The Peyook, or Guinea worm, the *dracunculus persarum* of Koempfer,* is found chiefly on the ſhores of the Perſian gulf, and in the ſouthern parts of Perſia; more eſpecially in the province of Carmania, and on the iſland of Ormuz. The origin and progreſs of the diſorder occaſioned by this ſingular worm, is deſcribed by Koempfer in his Amoenitates Exoticæ, with ſo much accuracy and ſpirit, that we hope to be pardoned in preſenting our readers with an extract from this valuable work, which, it is much to be regretted, has not hitherto been given to our countrymen in an Engliſh dreſs.†

* Vide Kœmpfer's Amœnitates Exoticæ, Fasciculus 3d, Observatio 4th, p. 529.

† In lucem prodituri nuncia plerumque est febricula, ut plurimum ephemera, non nunquam in tertiam diem protracta, cum fetæ partis rubidine et tumore; in quo postridie exsurgit postula pisi magnitudine, tenera, aquosa, pellucida, non raro atricolor: qua post unum aut alterum diem spontē ruptâ vel acu apertâ, prosilit lumbrici summus apex, sive rostellum, ibidem hactenus absconditum, quod pedetentim et reliquum corpus undecunque subsequitur, blandâ attractione quotidié solicitatum. Sæpè etiam non nisi prævïó partis dolore, et duritie vix sensibili nascitur; rupto ibidem, quo perpetuo sibi viam parat, ul-

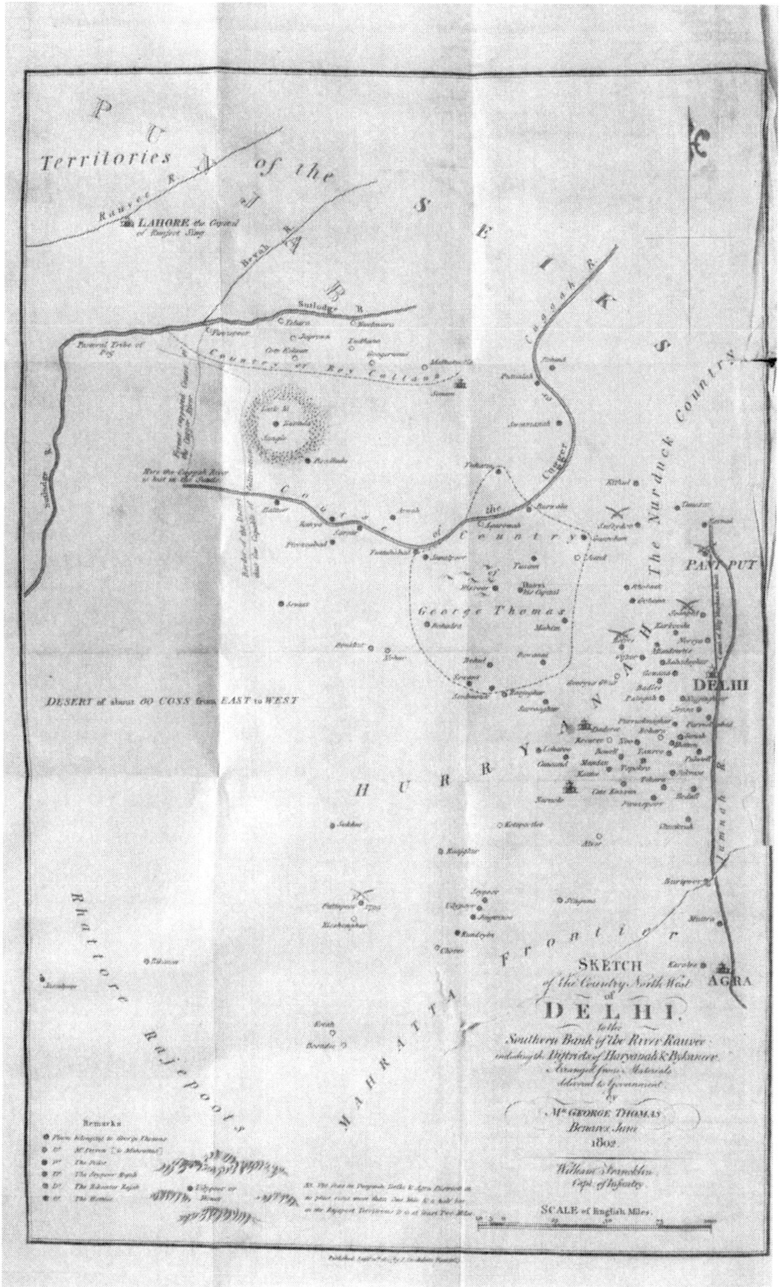
SKETCH
of the Country North West
of
DELHI,
to the
Southern Bank of the River Rauvee
including the Districts of Haryanah & Bikaneer
Arranged from Materials
delivered to Government
by
Mr. GEORGE THOMAS
Benares June
1802.
William Franklin
Capt. of Infantry
SCALE of English Miles.
Territories of the
SEIKS
LAHORE the Capital of Runjeet Sing
Rauvee R.
Beyah R.
Sutledge R.
Caggah R.
Country of Rey Cattaus
Country of the
George Thomas
HURRYANAH
The Nurduck Country
PANIPUT
DELHI
AGRA
Jumnah
DESERT of about 80 COSS from EAST to WEST
Rhattore Rajepoots
MAHRATTA Frontier
Remarks

The natives of Hurrianah for a ſucceſſion of ages having been in a conſtant ſtate of warfare,

cusculo, sine epidermidis pustula. Excretio pro lumbrici magnitudine et maturitate citiori, tum pro situ et loco generationis vario, facilior est aut difficilior, longior aut brevior: raro autem pariter et vivus, frequentissime successivo tempore, diebus circiter decem, extrahitur. Omnium felicissime egreditur, qui in scroti cavo absconditur, nam hunc, barba exerta, vivum illico educimus, sine dôlore et purulenti ulceris incommodo. Supra musculum aliquem in crure aut brachio non admodum dispersus jacens, vel in gyrum volutus, qualis oculo et tactu deprehenditur, intra paucos dies, a quo maturare incipit, sine notabili pure et molestia, quin vel uno interdum nisu extrahitur. Ex femore et ulnis plerumque facili partu exit, diebus admodum paucis. Sita vago ligamenta pedis involvens admodum difficulter, mora videlicet viginti vel amplius dierum, excluditur, cum tabo quotidie copiosissime magnoque ægroti cum dolore et incommodo.

The time when the worm is about to appear, is indicated by slight feverish symptoms in the patient; it is sometimes protracted until the third day, when the part is affected by a red tumor, which on the ensuing day becomes a pustule of a bright black: this breaking of itself, or being pierced with a needle, the head or snout of the worm makes its appearance, and as quickly withdraws itself from the touch. To extract the worm, great patience and caution are necessary, as from unskilfulness in handling it frequently breaks, which not only causes acute pain to possess great personal bravery; they are expert in the use of arms, particularly in the exercise

the patient, but the part remaining degenerates into an incurable ulcer. The time necessary for extracting this worm is longer or shorter, according to its size, but it is seldom taken out entire before the expiration of ten days. It sometimes lies dispersed above a muscle, at other times it is found in the interstices of the muscles of the legs and arms, or convoluted; it is laid hold of with an armed needle. A few days from the time in which it begins to maturate it may be extracted without pain or any considerable discharge of matter, except when it is withdrawn by a first attempt. From the thighs and arm-pits it makes an easy exit within a few days: when it appears among the tendons of the feet, great delay is experienced. It takes up twenty days in the operation, which is moreover attended with a copious discharge of matter, and severe pain to the patient.

The general mode adopted in India for the extraction of this worm, is by means of a small round piece of bamboo, to which is attached a thread. This being fixed to the worm, so much of the thread is wound round the body as to prevent its retiring again within the flesh. In this state it remains until the ensuing day, when a little more is added to the former, until the whole is extracted. By this curious process, it is easy to be perceived the extreme care that is necessary to prevent its breaking.

Travellers have at various times been afflicted with this disorder; for myself I never experienced it, though it was of the lance, ſabre, and the matchlock;* but though brave, they are in diſpoſition cruel, treacherous, and vindictive; and when engaged in domeſtic quarrels, ſcruple not to kill their antagoniſt on the ſlighteſt and moſt trivial occaſions.

For his capital, Mr. Thomas ſelected the town of Hanſi;† this place is ſituate ninety

common to the inhabitants of Persia, during my residence in that country, many years since. The spirited and intelligent Bruce got it after his return from Abyssinia to Grand Cairo. In like manner this worm is extracted from the negroes on the coast of Africa, who attribute the cause of this complaint to the badness of the water.

* Mr. Thomas adduced several instances of their desperate resolution, and almost invincible courage, once against the celebrated Ismaul Beg, at the town of Bhowanny, and a second time against the attacks of Gopaul Row, the Mahratta general. The army of the latter was defeated at Sanghee, after an unsuccessful siege of forty days.

In an assault against the fort of Deighle, Appakandarow, though attended by a select and well-appointed army, was repulsed with considerable loss.

† The subjoined schedule contains an account tolerably accurate of the country held by Mr. Thomas, including the

miles north-weſt of Delhi, and nearly in the centre of his newly-acquired domains. The town ſtanding upon a hill is peculiarly well adapted to a permanent reſidence.

No water can be procured within ſeven coſs, but the garriſon have an ample ſupply of that

names of the separate pergunnahs, the number of villages formerly inhabited, compared with its present state; the revenues, bearings, and distances of each pergunnah being taken from Hansi, the capital.

Pergunnahs.	Former number of villages.	Number of villages now inhabited.	Former Revenue.	Present Revenue.	Coss: bearing and distance from Hansi.
Hansi, - -	84	32	2,50,000	60,000	Coss.
Benwala, - -	46	11	63,000	11,000	14 N.
Tohana, - -	74	26	1,20,000	25,000	34 N.
Jemaulpore, - -	70	16	1,10,000	70,000	36 N. N. W.
Augrowa, - -	44	3	70,000	3,000	24 N. W.
Hassar, - -	250	13	3,00,000	10,000	12 W.
Bahra, - -	24	18	40,000	12,000	30 W. S. W.
Seedmuck, - -	70	4	30,000	6,000	24 S. W.
Sevance, - -	70	11	50,000	14,000	24 S.W. by S.
Tesam, - -	74	18	70,000	16,000	12 S.
Maheem, - -	24	16	50,000	23,000	16 E. S. E.
Safydoo, - -	24	8	30,000	10,000	36 E. N. E.
Jaind, - -	72	66	2,00,000	70,000	18 E. N. E.
Casohan, - -	24	11	50,000	16,000	24 N. E.
	950	253	14,30,000	2,86,000	
Held by Mr. G Thomas of the Mahrattas.					
Jiger, - -	250	90	3,00,000	80,000	40 E. S. E.
Byree, - -	24	16	30,000	14,000	35 E. S. E.
Maundotee, - -	24	11	30,000	10,000	44 E.
Pathoda, - -	4	4	1,00,000	10,000	51 S. E.
Badlee, - -	72	30	1,20,000	1,20,000	48 E. S. E.
Total	374	151	5,80,000	1,44,000	
Grand Total	1324	404	20,10,000	4,30,000	

neceſſary article from ſeveral wells within the fort. This circumſtance renders difficult an attack, except at the ſeaſon of the periodical rains. "Here," ſays Mr. Thomas, with that energy and ſpirited animation which diſtinguiſhed him throughout the ſcenes of his extraordinary life, "I eſtabliſhed my capital, "rebuilt the walls of the city, long ſince fallen "into decay, and repaired the fortifications. "As it had been long deſerted, at firſt I found "difficulty in procuring inhabitants, but by "degrees and gentle treatment I ſelected "between five and ſix thouſand perſons, to "whom I allowed every lawful indulgence.

"I eſtabliſhed a mint, and coined my own "rupees, which I made current in my army "and country; as from the commencement "of my career at Jyjur, I had reſolved to "eſtabliſh an independency, I employed work-"men and artificers of all kinds, and I now "judged that nothing but force of arms could "maintain me in my authority. I therefore "increaſed their numbers, caſt my own artil-"lery, commenced making muſquets, match-"locks, and powder; and, in ſhort, made the

" best preparations for carrying on an offen-
" five and defenfive war; till at length having
" gained a capital and country bordering on
" the Seik territories, I wifhed to put myfelf
" in a capacity, when a favorable opportunity
" fhould offer, of attempting the conqueft of
" the Punjab, and afpired to the honour of
" planting the Britifh ftandard on the banks
" of the Attock."*

* To carry his plans into effect, and for the support of his troops, Mr. Thomas appropriated a part of the revenue arising from the lands granted by the Mahrattas, and with much judgment and discernment, naturally inherent in liberal minds, endeavoured to conciliate the affections of his men by granting pensions to the widows and children or nearest relations of those soldiers who fell in his service. These pensions, amounting to 40,000 rupees per annum, were regularly paid to the respective claimants, a mode which reflects the highest credit on Mr. Thomas's character, but which had long since been anticipated by the wisdom of the British government in rewarding their veteran sepoys. The payments were made every six months, and the nearest relation of the deceased, whether officer or soldier, received the half pay of his rank. This and the expence of casting cannon, the fabrication of small arms, and purchase of warlike stores, consumed that part of Mr. Thomas's revenues which he derived from the districts granted him by the Mahrattas, as detailed in the foregoing schedule.

CHAPTER VII.

Reflections.—Mr. Thomas resolves to invade the Jypoor territory.—Geographical and statistical account of that country.—Revenues, history, manners and customs of the inhabitants.

HAVING accompanied Mr. Thomas through a series of services, as interesting in their nature as singular in their result; having beheld him from the situation of a fugitive, a friendless and deserted object, now by the force of his own exertions, and an intrepidity of spirit scarcely to be paralleled, obtain a situation seldom equalled by the most fortunate; we must next proceed to trace the causes and describe the progress of those events which led to a decline of his authority, and in the end, as the only means of safety and escape from the persecution of numerous and inveterate foes, compelled him to seek an asylum in the territories of his native sovereign.

Not however to anticipate the order of events, it will now be neceſſary to recur to Mr. Thomas's ſituation when in poſſeſſion of his newly acquired country. His mind having been long intent on the reduction of the Punjab, he would now have ſet out on this intereſting expedition, but on a review of his troops made for the purpoſe, he found his force inſufficient to the taſk, and was therefore induced to have recourſe to an excurſion into the Jypore dominions, which had hitherto afforded a never-failing ſupply to his neceſſities, and whoſe ruler was in conſequence become his bitter enemy.

The ſituation of the Jypore dominions, and their relative importance among the ſtates of Rajpootana, will juſtify a detail of the ſtrength and internal reſources of this intereſting country. The dominions of Jypore are nearly one hundred coſs from north to ſouth, and fifty from eaſt to weſt; they are bounded on the north by the diſtrict of Hurrianah, on the north-eaſt by Alvar, eaſt by Karolee and Bhurtpoor, ſouth by Kota, Boondee and Mewar, ſouth-weſt by Kiſhenghur, weſt by Ajmere and Joud-pore, and on the north-weſt by the country of Beykaneer.

The eastern, north-eastern, southern and south-western parts of Jypore produce wheat, cotton, tobacco, and in general whatever is common to other parts of India; to which may be added, excellent cattle, and abundance of good copper.

The country in general is watered from the wells: the northern and north-western districts being sandy are not so well supplied with this necessary article as the midland parts; but in that part of Jypore which is mountainous, the streams that issue from thence are of the highest advantage to the cultivation of the soil.

The Rajpoots of Jypore are not esteemed so brave as those of Joudpore, for which Mr. Thomas imagines three causes may be ascribed:—first, the encroachments of the prince on the feudal system, which obtained formerly in this country, and which has contributed to render the people abject and slavish; second, that their armies are commanded by people whom they neither love, fear, or respect; and thirdly, the difference of climate, which is particularly obſervable in a compariſon with the ſtature and perſonal comelineſs of the Rhatores with thoſe of Jypore, the inhabitants of the former being by far more robuſt in their make.

No Rajpoot engages in trade, or any mechanical occupation whatſoever: they are all, without exception, either ſoldiers or huſbandmen.

They are of a high and unconquerable ſpirit, and do not think poverty any diſhonour: on the contrary they will often aſſert in converſation, that provided a perſon ſhall conduct himſelf with propriety towards his neighbours, he, whether poſſeſſed of riches or not, is, in all reſpects, to be conſidered as a man of perfect honour.

Among other cuſtoms peculiar to the Rajpoots the preſervation of female honour holds with them a ſuperior ſtation; ſcandal uttered againſt the wife or daughter of a Rajpoot is never forgiven, and death alone can expiate the offence.

This high ſenſe of honour has, however, rendered them of all other people moſt circumſpect in converſation, and they are careful of giving offence; ſhould a Rajpoot ſuſpect a perſon inclined to ſlight him, he will not only forego every proſpect of advantage to be derived from the uſual mode of reconciliation, by the mutual exertion of common friends, but will even make a circuitous route to avoid paſſing by the habitation of his antagoniſt. This ſeverity of manners may appear to ſtrangers, at a firſt view, to be prohibitory; but a long reſidence in the country, and intimate acquaintance with the manners and cuſtoms of this extraordinary people, have long ſince convinced Mr. Thomas that a perſon of upright manners cannot aſſociate with a better companion than a Rajpoot.

In their marriages they pay the ſtricteſt attention to caſt, and will never unite themſelves with people of inferior condition; this is ſo unavoidably neceſſary, that were a man to enter into an alliance with a family of ignoble blood, the children of ſuch marriage would in conſequence be deprived of their right of inheritance; a ſtriking inſtance of national pertinacity.

A plurality of wives, though allowed by their inſtitutions, excepting among the higher order of Rajpoots, is ſeldom practiſed; and even in that inſtance it is more owing to motives of policy than inclination, and ariſes chiefly from a deſire of extinguiſhing thoſe antient feuds which have ſo long ſubſiſted among families.

During their infancy and childhood, the Rajpoot women being kept in a conſtant ſtate of concealment, when once married are ſeldom ſeen but by the very neareſt in blood among their own relations. This cuſtom is ſo rooted among them, that a lady would conſider herſelf as diſhonoured by any expoſure of her perſon to public view.

This ſecluſion of females in ſouthern Aſia, has been erroneouſly ſuppoſed by many perſons to be a hardſhip on the ſex; but, in Mr. Thomas's opinion, it is underſtood in a ſenſe rather too general; in every other reſpect, the Rajpoot character yields to no nation in Aſia, or perhaps in the world, in maintaining the ties of relationſhip and conſanguinity, by a ſeries of the kindeſt actions towards each other. They are dutiful ſons, kind huſbands, and affectionate brothers.

The men, it is true, are in the higheſt degree jealous of their honour, but the exempting their women from perſonal labour, in employing them though ſecreted from the reſt of the world, in ſuperintending the education of their children, and other domeſtic avocations, cannot ſurely with juſtice be conſidered as a hardſhip. "And "if we look," ſays Mr. Thomas, "at the con-"dition of the inferior ſort of women in moſt "parts of Europe, the ſituation of the Rajpoot "females may be, perhaps, beneficed by the "compariſon."

One cuſtom, and one alone, obtains among this infatuated people, at which nature muſt ever revolt, and humanity ſhudder: it is the practice of putting to death their new-born females. In other reſpects tender and affectionate towards their offspring, it was a matter of extreme ſurprize to Mr. Thomas that in this inſtance the Rajpoots ſhould ſo far exceed the bounds of natural affection.

From motives of curioſity, he was induced to demand their reaſon for allowing of this horrid practice; the reply in general was, "it is our cuſtom;" but when Mr. Thomas remarked that was but a bad plea for the commiſſion of the horrid crime of murder, they would then urge the poſſibility of their daughters meeting with bad huſbands, who might hereafter bring diſgrace and diſhonour on their poſterity; or, that the infants themſelves might, at ſome future period, commit actions unworthy of the name of Rajpoots. "Should this reaſoning hold," ſaid Mr. Thomas, "and the Rajpoot "nation, in this particular, were to be all of "the ſame mind, they would in the ſpace of "one hundred years, or much leſs time, become "extinct." This argument enforced with pertinacity, had, for a time, the effect of carrying apparent conviction of the impropriety of a cuſtom ſo unnatural, and he had the ſatisfaction to obtain frequent promiſes from ſome reſpectable families in that country, that they would diſcontinue the practice in future. This promiſe he afterwards learnt had, in ſome inſtances, among their own relations been happily carried into effect.

With theſe exceptions the Rajpoots may be conſidered as honourable, brave, and faithful; and few nations who are not in poſſeſſion of the advantages of education, or thoſe benefits which ariſe from the refinements of civilized life, can be ſaid to be poſſeſſed of more good qualities, or benevolence of diſpoſition.

This benevolence of diſpoſition is exhibited in a peculiar manner towards the Jauts, who are cultivators of the ſoil, for though the Rajpoots keep them under the ſtricteſt obedience, and do not allow them more than is neceſſary for their ſubſiſtence, deprive them of the honour of bearing arms, except it be on the actual invaſion of their frontiers; notwithſtanding theſe circumſtances, apparently ſo degrading, the farmer acknowledges that he lives happily under the government, and that his ſtate of poverty is, by the mildneſs in manners exhibited towards him by his ſuperiors the Rajpoots, converted into content.

The rajah of Jypore, rich in resources of every kind, is in fact a very powerful prince; his cavalry may be computed at not less than thirty thousand men. He has twelve thousand infantry in his service, exclusive of five or six thousand mercenaries. In this statement are not included the aids which he would be enabled to draw from his connections with the neighbouring countries of Joudpore, Oudepore, and Beykaneer, to whose rulers he is allied by blood. His artillery is numerous, and well-appointed, "and in short," says Mr. Thomas, "an alliance with this prince, in case of necessity, may be one day deemed not unworthy the precaution and foresight of the British government in Asia."

One thing only tends to mark a deficiency in the otherwise sound policy of this prince, which is, the appointment of people of inferior rank to high commands in his army.

Naturally high-spirited and haughty, a Rajpoot is, of all other people, most averse to serve under a person whom he considers his inferior.

Hence arifes the impolicy of the rajah, who has of late years introduced into commands in his army, fervants, mechanics, and even flaves. Thefe men, deftitute of talents or conduct, cannot be fuppofed to poffefs that independancy of fpirit which alone excites to the performance of great actions. In juftification of the rajah's meafures in this inftance, it has however been afferted by fome, that the difference of caft and condition makes none in refpect to courage: which Mr. Thomas obferves may hold good with refpect to European troops, or even Indian troops difciplined and conducted by European officers, as, in that inftance, they may be confidered as a machine actuated and animated by the voice of the commander; but in an Indian army, where difcipline never exifted, little can be expected from chiefs who in their actions are not ftimulated by a fenfe of perfonal honour.

The Rajpoots, therefore, who compofed the greater number of the troops in the Jypore army, deeming thefe commanders inadequate to perform the duties of their ftation, became confequently indifferent in their acknowledgement of authority: theſe men, moreover, from a conſtant reſidence at the court of a gay and luxurious prince, for ſuch is the character of the reigning ſovereign, have aſſumed the manners of courtiers, and indulge in too frequent ridicule on the plain and honeſt ſimplicity of Rajpoot manners; while the latter, from their haughtineſs of ſpirit, and the diſguſt conceived at this treatment, never fail, on the ſlighteſt token of diſreſpect, to revenge the inſult, by putting the aggreſſor to inſtant death.

Among the recreations of the Kutchwah Rajpoots, the exerciſe on horſeback forms a diſtinguiſhing feature. If ever, by chance, they ſhould be neceſſitated to combat on foot, it is only in defence of their houſes and families. Their arms conſiſt of a lance and ſabre; and though the rajah, of late years, has introduced the muſquet and matchlock, they make but little uſe of theſe weapons. They have, in common with other Rajpoots, a thick quilted jacket, which, like armour, will reſiſt with effect the ſtroke of a ſcymeter.

The country of Jypore is capable of yielding

an annual revenue of one hundred and twenty lacks of rupees; though from the nature of its government, the amount paid into the rajah's treasury now seldom exceeds sixty lacks. This may be accounted for by considering that the feudal system prevailing throughout the dominions of Jypore lessens thereby the actual revenue of the state. The respective chieftains hold their lands in Jâiedad, and for the express purpose of affording a body of troops in times of emergency, which cannot be dispensed with. To this certain expence are to be added the occasional exactions of the sovereign upon particular chiefs, and consequent diminution of the effective military force.

The chiefs of the district termed Sheckhawathy in particular, who in former times could contribute their quota towards the exigencies of the state, by bringing ten thousand men into the field, and who from great military experience and length of service, were justly considered as the best soldiers in the Jypore army, can now with difficulty muster three thousand men. Of late years these troops have become not only extremely disgusted with the service, occasioned by the causes already detailed, but have evinced a spirit of discontent and dissatisfaction, which in the event of civil discord threatens to prove highly detrimental to the general interests of the community.

The Rajpoot princes of Jypore are of the tribe called Kutchwa, and tracing their origin from a remote antiquity, this illustrious family in the annals of the empire are called Beni Suruj, or children of the sun. They originally settled in the southern parts of the province of Gualior, and drew their lineage from rajah Ramchunder, a prince of high celebrity.

It appears from the Hindoo books called Ramayoon and Muhubhârat, that rajah Ramchunder had two sons, the one named Nubh, and the other Koosh. The descendants of the former are denominated Burhagoojer, and those of the latter Kutchwayah. Pirthi Raj* the

* Pirthi Sing, aforementioned, was the founder of a dynasty, denominated Duazdah Kutchoory, or the twelve partitions; so called from the number of his sons, among whom, to prevent animosities, he during his lifetime divided his dominions into as many separate parts.

first sovereign who mounted the throne of Jypore, in the æra of Bekermajeet,* 1550, died in 1584.

The descendants of the Rajahs of Ambeer having established themselves in the finest parts of the peninsula, for a series of years were possessed of high authority and extensive dominion. Among these Maun Sing, a prince renowned in the annals of the empire, assumed a leading part; others, following his example, in succession contributed to the permanent establishment of their family, by acts of no less wisdom than benevolence.

The dry and uninteresting matter contained in a genealogical detail can be gratifying to none; it will therefore be sufficient to remark, that the succession of the Rajpoot princes from their founder continued for several centuries to fill the throne of Jypore; and our present detail will conclude by observing, that in the records of the royal family of Ambeer, there

* For the æra of Bekermajeet consult Mr. Gladwin's Ayeen Akbery.

exists a table of two hundred and fifteen princes from rajah Ramchunder to Purtaub Sing, the present sovereign.*

* In the foregoing detail the compiler has great satisfaction in offering his best thanks to Colonel Palmer, late ambassador at the Poonah Durbar; to Captain John Baillie, professor of the Arabic and Persian languages; and to the gentlemen students in the Persian and Arabic classes in the college of Fort William, founded under the auspices of his excellency the most noble Marquis Wellesley: Colonel Palmer having most obligingly communicated to him some M.S. matter on the genealogy of the Rajpoot princes of Jypore, Joudpore, and Oudipore; and Captain Baillie having, with no less kindness, suggested to his pupils the translation of it as a voluntary exercise during their vacation hours.

CHAPTER VIII.

In an expedition against Jypore, Mr. Thomas is joined by Vavon Row.—Their proceedings.—Account of the city of Futtahpore.—Approach of the Jypore army.—Battle of Futtahpore.

IN returning from a digreſſion, which it is hoped will have afforded our readers ſome relief from the tedium of narrative detail, it is now neceſſary to remark, that about this time Luckwah, commander in chief of the forces of Scindiah north of the Nerbuddah, ſent orders to Vavon Row to invade Jypore; and in his letter on that ſubject, having mentioned the ſum exacted by his predeceſſors in office from each of the diſtricts, he recommended Vavon Row to demand an equal proportion on the preſent occaſion, as a reward for the ſervice to be performed: he moreover allowed Vavon Row ten annas in the rupee, from the money thus collected, to be divided among the troops, and the remaining ſix annas to be ſent to his own treaſury.

Vavon Row, on receipt of the above order, wrote preſſing letters to Mr. Thomas, inviting him to join in the propoſed expedition; but he, though willing to make a temporary incurſion to Jypore to obtain preſent relief to his neceſſities, was by no means inclined to go the lengths propoſed, and at firſt from prudential motives declined the offer.

Mr. Thomas moreover was not ignorant that the ſubſiſtence of ſo large a body of troops on an expedition like the preſent, could only be obtained by a full treaſury, and his own reſources were at preſent dried up. That the numerous cavalry which the Jypore rajah could bring into the field would very much impede their efforts in procuring the neceſſary ſupplies of forage and proviſions; and that without theſe aids the ſucceſs of the expedition would be very doubtful; and finally, he remarked to Vavon Row, that even if ſucceſs attended their arms the rajah would never pay to them the ſum ſpecified, but would refer the matter to Luckwah himſelf, whereby they would loſe the fruits of their labours. Theſe ſuggeſtions, however ſalutary in their deſign, could not perſuade Vavon Row to give up his ſcheme, or convince him that their united force was incompetent to the preſent conteſt.

That chief now ſent his vakeel to Mr. Thomas, promiſing him a ſum of money, of which he ſtood in great need, for the proffered aſſiſtance, and he at length cloſed with the propoſal.

His force at this time conſiſted of three battalions of four hundred men each, with fourteen pieces of artillery, ninety horſe, three hundred Rohillas, and two hundred of the peaſantry of Hurrianah, with which he joined Vavon Row at Kanond.

That chief had himſelf one battalion of infantry, four pieces of artillery, nine hundred cavalry, and ſix hundred irregulars. With this force they commenced their march towards Jypore. On entering the country, a party of the Rajah's troops ſtationed to collect the revenues retreated; when the chief of the diſtrict ſent vakeels into Mr. Thomas's camp, who agreed to the payment of the two years' tribute which had been named by Luckwah.

The offer was accepted, and the troops marching forward compelled ſeveral others to ſubmit to ſimilar exactions. For near a month the united armies continued their progreſs without interruption; but the rajah of Jypore, who had in the interim been collecting his troops, now marched to the relief of his poſſeſſions, with a reſolution to puniſh the invaders, and revenge the inſult he had ſuſtained, by giving battle wherever he ſhould meet with his enemies. The army thus collected, amounted to forty thouſand men, with which the rajah marched againſt Mr. Thomas and Vavon Row, who, not having yet got poſſeſſion of any place from whence a ſupply of grain could be drawn, became ſenſible of their error, and were reduced to a ſituation truly hazardous. Vavon Row deeming it impoſſible to encounter ſo large a force, now acquainted Mr. Thomas that he muſt rely on his own exertions; that from the numbers and acknowledged bravery of the enemy, who were chiefly Rajpoots, there could exiſt but ſmall hope of ſucceſs in riſking an engagement, and for theſe conſiderations adviſed Mr. Thomas to retreat. To combat theſe arguments, and fruſtrate a deſign ſo puſillanimous in its nature, Mr. Thomas reminded Vavon Row of his haſty and inconſiderate conduct in leading them into their preſent exigency, that there exiſted no cauſe to prevent at leaſt one trial of ſtrength, their own troops being faithful to them, and in high ſpirit to engage; that moreover, to think of a retreat on the preſent occaſion, without an exertion on their part, would be a diſhonour to himſelf and his progenitors, who never turned their backs on an enemy; and finally obſerved, that if Vavon Row now receded, he never could again expect to be employed by Scindiah, or any other chief under his authority. Theſe arguments combined at length made an impreſſion on the mind of Vavon Row, and he agreed to riſk an engagement.

With this determination, they marched forthwith to the city of Futtahporè, in which they expected to meet with a supply of grain sufficient for the consumption of their troops; but on their arrival the inhabitants, who had received intimation of their approach, were busily employed in filling up the wells in the neighbourhood, in order to distress the troops for water. They had nearly completed this design, only one remaining open, when Mr. Thomas arrived.

The possession of this remaining well now became the object of contention betwixt Mr. Thomas and a body of four hundred men who had been detached from the city for the express purpose of filling it up. Mr. Thomas, who perceived no time was to be lost, ordered his cavalry to charge. The action was at first obstinate; but two of the enemy's sirdars being killed, the rest retreated, and the well was happily preserved. This was of great importance, as except in this single supply no water was to be procured but from a considerable distance.

The service on this day was uncommonly severe, as Mr. Thomas had completed a march of five-and-twenty miles over a deep sand, which in most places was above the ancles of his men; he was therefore glad to encamp, and afford some repose to his fatigued troops.

As the city of Futtahpore was marked in Mr. Thomas's military career, as a place of signal success, an account of it may not perhaps be deemed intrusive.

Kaieem Khan, a Tartar nobleman, accompanied the standard of the Moguls on their first invasion of Hindostan; and as a reward for his military services on that occasion had been presented with the government of the adjoining country of Hurrianah and Jinjinnoo, where he settled with his family and adherents.

In process of time, however, the Mogul princes who sat on the throne of Delhi, unmindful of the services of this illustrious family, endeavoured to effect their ruin; and finally by a tyrannical procedure, expelled them from the province. On their expulsion they sought an asylum in the dominions of Jypore, by whose ruler they were kindly received, and where they remained until the present time. The city of Futtahpore was allotted for their reſidence: where, ſince that period, the deſcendants of Kaieem Khan have continued to reſide, retaining, along with the name of their founder, the characteriſtic energy and military ſpirit of the tribe; and are to this day termed by the natives *Kaieem Khanee*, or deſcendants of Kaieem Khan.

The city of Futtahpore being full of people, Mr. Thomas, in order to ſave the effuſion of blood, was deſirous to treat with the inhabitants for its ranſom; but the demands of Vavon Row were ſo exorbitant, that they declined compliance.

The Mahratta chief aſked no leſs a ſum than ten lacs of rupees, whilſt the townspeople only offered one, encouraged perhaps by the hope of receiving aſſiſtance from the rajah of Jypore, who was rapidly advancing to their relief.

During theſe negotiations night came on, and nothing was done reſpecting the propoſed ranſom: ſome perſons, however, who had been ſent into the city by Mr. Thomas to protect the place until they could make the terms of ſurrender, unluckily began to plunder the inhabitants; which circumſtance ſo exaſperated the commandant, that he broke off all further treaty, and the united force then took poſſeſſion of the place by ſtorm. This was ſcarcely effected, when intelligence of the rajah's approach was announced to Mr. Thomas, who then thought proper to fortify his camp, which he did in the following manner. In the neighbourhood were abundance of large thorn-trees, which are common in the weſt of India: a ſufficient number of theſe were cut down, and, by Mr. Thomas's direction, piled one upon another in the front and flanks of his camp, his rear being ſecured by the city of Futtahpore. To render it more impenetrable, the branches of the trees* being cloſely interwoven

* It is remarkable that Mr. Thomas, who had read very little, should, from the resources of his own mind, have adopted a mode of defence parallel with one related in the History of Modern Europe. Speaking of the approach of the British army under the command of General Abercromby, in the war of 1758, against the fort of Ticonderago, in North America, "The French (says the historian)

with each other, were then made faſt with ropes, thus forming *chevaux de frize* to keep off the cavalry; and laſtly a large quantity of ſand was thrown between the branches which pointed outwards toward the enemy.

A trench could not be dug, as the ſand was ſo looſe in its quality that the excavations were inſtantly filled up as ſoon as made: but the abbatis above-mentioned was on ſeveral accounts highly ſerviceable, particularly as it not only ſecured Mr. Thomas from the attacks of the enemy's cavalry, but afforded protection to the camp. He next directed batteries to be made for the defence of the different wells in the neighbourhood, which had by this time been cleaned out and opened afreſh for uſe. He took poſſeſſion of and fortified the city in the beſt manner that the ſhortneſs of the time

" were stationed under the cannon of the place, behind an " *abbatis* or breast-work formed of the trunks of trees " piled one upon another; and they were farther defended " by whole trees, with their branches outward, some of " which were cut and sharpened so as to answer the pur- " pose of *chevaux de frize*."—See Russel's History of Modern Europe, vol. v. p. 288.

admitted; ordered a large ſupply of proviſions to be brought into his camp; and had ſcarcely finiſhed theſe preparations, when the vanguard of the enemy's army appeared in ſight.

On their arrival, the enemy encamped within four coſs of Mr. Thomas, and ſoon after puſhed on a detachment of cavalry and infantry to clear the wells in the neighbourhood. For two days he allowed them to proceed with their work uninterruptedly; but on the third morning, he with two battalions of infantry, eight pieces of artillery, and his own cavalry, marched out with a reſolution to attack their grand park of artillery, leaving directions to the battalion that remained behind to attack and diſperſe the advanced party before-mentioned. On his departure, he left a written paper for Vavon Row, requeſting that chief to follow with the remainder of his cavalry, and with the infantry which he had with him, to provide for the ſecurity of the camp.

Mr. Thomas was diſpoſed to act in this manner from his experience of the Mahrattas, who he well knew, if acquainted with his plans, could keep nothing ſecret, but would, by divulging them, put the enemy on their guard. It was night when he ſet out; and a tumbril being upſet on the road, occaſioned conſiderable delay in their progreſs, ſo that the day began to dawn before the evil was repaired; and, to add to his mortification, on arriving near the camp, he perceived the enemy aſſembled under arms, and ready to receive him.

It was now too late to carry his firſt deſign into execution. He puſhed on, however; and, coming up with a party who now advanced to meet him, attacked them to the number of ſeven thouſand men with great ſpirit and vigour. The enemy made but a feeble reſiſtance, and ſoon after withdrew to their main body, having ſuſtained conſiderable loſs. The wells which had been cleaned out were again filled up; and Mr. Thomas, after collecting the horſes and other cattle which had been left on the field, returned with his detachment to camp. On his way he met with the Mahratta cavalry, who ſeemed much out of humour that they had not been conſulted on ſo important an occaſion: but Vavon

Row, their chief, repreſſed their pride by telling them plainly, that their own delay in accoutring was the real cauſe of their diſappointment.

Mr. Thomas's officers now received khilluts* from the Mahratta chief; and, to prevent animoſities, ſimilar marks of honour were beſtowed, though with reluctance, on the officers of the Mahratta horſe.

Preparations were now making by the enemy to bring on a general engagement, which proved far greater in its conſequences than either party had foreſeen. The next morning at day-break, Mr. Thomas was informed that there was a great buſtle in the enemy's camp, and ſhortly after received intelligence of their actual approach in order of battle. He had determined in his own mind the ſpot where he would engage; and as he well knew no reliance could be placed on the Mahrattas, he was neceſſitated to leave a part of his infantry, and four ſix-pounders, to guard

* Dresses of honour.

the camp and cover his rear, which was in danger of being ſurrounded by the enemy: with the remainder, conſiſting of two battalions of infantry, two hundred Rohillas, his cavalry, and ten pieces of artillery, he prepared for the encounter.

The Mahrattas, on ſeeing the immenſe force they had to cope with, gave themſelves over for loſt; and Mr. Thomas was in a manner compelled to fight this important battle without aſſiſtance.

After ſome manœuvres on either ſide, he was glad to find that the enemy diſtributed their army as he wiſhed.

Their right wing, conſiſting of the whole force of the Rajpoot cavalry, was deſtined to the attack of his camp; and ſo certain were they of victory, that, on perceiving the ſtockade we have before deſcribed, they laughed at the idea that *a few buſhes*, as they were pleaſed to term them, could for a moment retard their progreſs, or reſiſt the impetuoſity of the attack. The left wing, conſiſting of four thouſand Rohillas, three thousand Ghosseins, and six thousand irregular infantry, commanded by the chiefs of their respective districts, advanced at the same time with hasty strides and loud shouts, to take possession of the city, the loss of which, by cutting off the supply of water, would have been attended with the most serious consequences.

Their third, or main body, was composed of ten battalions of infantry, twenty-two pieces of artillery, and the *sillah posh*, or body guard, of the rajah, consisting of sixteen hundred men armed with matchlocks and sabres, and commanded by Rajah Roorojee Khavies, as generalissimo of the army. Notwithstanding this immense force, Mr. Thomas derived great advantage from the position in which his troops were drawn up; his front and flanks being secured by the fortified camp, and his rear by the city of Futtahpore.

The enemy's cavalry now advancing in close and compact order, the Mahrattas, who were posted in the rear, sent to require a reinforcement; and accordingly Mr. Thomas, though he could ill ſpare it, ordered four companies and two of the guns which had been left for the protection of the camp, to march out and join him; while, with three guns and five companies of infantry, he advanced to repel the attack of the enemy's horſe. His main body was commanded by John Morris, an Engliſhman, "who, though a brave man (ſays "Mr. Thomas), was better adapted to con-"duct a forlorn hope than to direct the mo-"tions of troops in a field of battle." Mr. Thomas having taken poſſeſſion of a very high ſand-bank, the enemy were thus placed between two fires, and could neither charge him or attack the camp; they conſequently began to draw off: but perceiving he had but few cavalry, and thoſe being in his rear, on a ſudden made a furious charge upon them, by which the perſon who commanded, and ſeveral other brave men, were inſtantly cut to pieces; and it was not until the advance of two companies of grenadiers, who, after having given their volley, charged with bayonets, that the enemy, thus expoſed, were compelled to retreat; and had the other diviſions of their army behaved with equal ſpirit, the day would have been their own. It was not, however, until their cavalry retreated, that the body destined to take possession of the city thought proper to advance a second time, having already once been driven back with considerable loss. Within the city Mr. Thomas had posted the Hurrianah infantry, and one hundred Rohillas, who, having fortified the highest and the strongest of the houses, could maintain themselves against all attacks, excepting those of artillery. Of this circumstance the enemy were aware; and accordingly now detached six pieces of cannon against the city, with orders to renew the combat. Mr. Thomas, on seeing their cavalry draw off from the field, was thereby enabled to succour those. He attacked the enemy instantly, and with so much vigour, that he compelled them to withdraw the artillery, and retreat. Their main body had by this time become a confused mass, without order, regularity, or method. The enemy, notwithstanding, was determined to risk the issue of the day on a general charge on Mr. Thomas's main body. But their general was not met on this occasion with equal ardour by his troops; and Mr. Thomas, perceiving them at a ſtand, commenced a heavy fire of grape ſhot from his guns, when, after ſuſtaining much loſs, the enemy retreated, and Mr. Thomas at this time ordered his battalions that had ſuffered the leaſt in the late conflict to advance in the purſuit. This, however, could not now be effected: the bullocks attached to the artillery, having been ſtationed behind a ſand-bank in the rear, could not be brought up with the expedition the emergency of the caſe required. At this time the Mahratta cavalry, who, during the preceding part of the conflict, had ſtood aloof, came forward with their ſervices in this purſuit. After ſome delay, Mr. Thomas, having procured a ſufficient number of bullocks for one of his guns, advanced with that and a battalion of infantry againſt the enemy; while the Mahratta horſe, to wipe off the diſgrace they had before ſuffered by their inactivity, joined in the purſuit.

The enemy were retreating in all directions; and Mr. Thomas prepared to take poſſeſſion of a pair of twenty-four pounders, which remained near the ſpot where he ſtood, and directed ſome of his people to carry them into the rear. At this inſtant a large body of Rajpoot cavalry advanced ſword in hand to reſcue the guns, when the cowardly Mahrattas, without ſuſtaining a ſingle aſſault, quitted the field. Mr. Thomas, perceiving the enemy continued to advance, drew up his troops as well as the ſhortneſs of time permitted; but before he was completely formed, the Mahratta horſe, in their puſillanimous flight, had broken through his left wing, and were followed cloſely by the Rajpoots, who began to cut down a great number of his men. Theſe gallant ſoldiers made a brave reſiſtance; many of them, even in the agonies of death, ſeized hold of the bridles of the enemy's horſes. The moment was critical; and to Mr. Thomas pregnant with future miſchief. With the only gun that remained, which he loaded up to the muzzle, and about one hundred and fifty of his followers, who bravely determined to conquer or die with him, he waited the event with fortitude. After permitting the enemy to approach within forty yards, he gave his fire, accompanied at the ſame time by a volley of muſquetry, with ſuch conſiderable effect, that great numbers of the enemy were inſtantly knocked down. This first effort, being followed by two other discharges, completely routed the enemy, and drove them from this well-contested field.

The Mahratta horse, who had been the chief cause of the late disaster, had in the interim hastened to the camp for protection, but were by Mr. Thomas's order refused admittance; and a small party of Rajpoots, who had followed in their rear, put several to death without mercy.*

The enemy's infantry, perceiving the attack made by the horse, began by this time to rally, and seemed inclined to renew the action. To afford them an opportunity of so doing, Mr. Thomas, having collected the remains of his gallant detachment, waited the attack. The day approaching to a close, the enemy thought proper to retire; and Mr. Thomas, after searching in vain for the twenty-four pounders which he had once possessed during the action, re-

* Throughout the whole of this action, Mr. Thomas speaks in terms most indignant of the disgraceful behaviour of his allies.

turned with his army to camp. In this action, in killed and wounded, Mr. Thomas lost three hundred men (amongst the latter of whom was the gallant Morris); that of the enemy amounted to more than two thousand, exclusive of horses and other valuable effects, which they were compelled to leave behind on the field of battle.

CHAPTER IX.

Military operations continued.—Mr. Thomas compelled to retreat.—Diſtreſs of the army.—Peace concluded.—Mr. Thomas marches againſt the rajah of Beykaneer.—Geographical deſcription of that country—of the Lackhi Jungle.—Military operations.—Mr. Thomas enters into engagements with Ambajee.

ON the enſuing morning, Mr. Thomas notified to the enemy's general that he might ſend proper perſons to bury the dead, and carry away the wounded men without interruption on his part. This civility was received with attention, accompanied at the ſame time with a requeſt to treat for peace.

Vavon Row, as a previous ſtipulation, inſiſted on the payment of a large ſum of money to indemnify him for loſſes ſuſtained during the campaign. To this the other objected, upon the principle of not being authoriſed by the rajah of Jypoor to disburse so large a sum without further orders. On receiving this answer, Mr. Thomas, suspecting that the enemy only waited for time to procure a reinforcement, recommended to Vavon Row the prosecution of hostilities. That chief was averse to the proposal, as he deemed the performance of mamla, or agreement, preferable to the hazard and risk of a second engagement, and therefore he overruled Mr. Thomas's objections. The negotiations for peace were therefore broken off. The enemy, having collected the scattered remains of their forces, took post on their former ground. In the mean time letters from Scindiah arrived, requesting Vavon Row to desist from hostilities against the troops of Jypoor. Others of similar import came from Mr. Perron, who had lately succeeded General Duboigne in the chief command of Scindiah's forces.

The enemy now of their own accord offered to pay the sum of fifty thousand rupees, which being most unaccountably rejected, Vavon Row had much reason to repent. During the late negotiations considerable reinforcements had arrived in the Jypoor camp, and hostilities recommenced with redoubled vigour on both ſides.

Mr. Thomas's troops from a want of forage, which they were obliged to collect from a diſtance of twenty miles from the camp, ſuſtained much inconvenience. In attempts to bring it in they were moreover haraſſed by detached parties of the enemy; and to complete their diſtreſs, the rajah of Beykaneer had by this time reinforced the Jypore army with five thouſand men. The Mahrattas in Mr. Thomas's camp, wholly uſeleſs, were fit only to plunder and deſtroy the unreſiſting peaſantry. Thus ſituated, and forage continuing to decreaſe, a council of war was held between Vavon Row, Mr. Thomas, and the other commanders, in which it was unanimouſly agreed to attempt a retreat to their own country.

Agreeably to this reſolution, the next morning before day-break, the troops began to file off, but were ſcarcely got in motion when the enemy's whole force came up to the attack. While it continued dark, great confuſion prevailed; but on the appearance of day-light, Mr.

Thomas, having formed his men, compelled the enemy to retreat with great loſs.

They ſtill continued to hang on his rear, and annoy him with the fire of artillery, aſſiſted by an immenſe quantity of rockets. From the rapidity of his march the enemy's heavy guns were ſoon obliged to remain behind, and the rocket and the matchlock men alone continued the purſuit. The day was intenſely hot, and the troops ſuffered ſeverely from a total want of water; this cauſe, however, operating in a ſimilar manner upon the enemy, prevented the execution of their plans. The ſervice was ſevere, and in the higheſt degree fatiguing; at length after a toilſome march, Mr. Thomas arrived in the evening at a village, where he fortunately met with two wells, containing plenty of excellent water. His men, eager to catch a refreſhing draught, crowded ſo faſt upon each other that two fell into the well, by which accident one of them was inſtantly ſuffocated, and the other with much difficulty brought out alive. Care was now taken to prevent a renewal of ſimilar accidents, by ſtationing an armed force to protect the well, till by degrees moſt of the troops having received a ſmall ſupply, the confuſion ceaſed, and order was reſtored in the camp.

The enemy ſtill followed in the rear, and encamped within two coſs. Mr. Thomas determined to renew the attack the enſuing day.

Mr. Thomas, perceiving that his men had loſt their accuſtomed ſpirits, to encourage them marched himſelf, on foot, at their head, during the whole of the enſuing day.

The enemy frequently appearing inclined to charge, Mr. Thomas directed the commandant of artillery to keep up a conſtant fire in the rear. This, in ſome degree checked their ardour, and afforded an opportunity to his own troops to move on. After a ſecond day's march, attended by circumſtances of diſtreſs ſimilar to the preceding one, though with conſiderable loſs to the enemy, Mr. Thomas arrived at a large town ; in the neighbourhood of which he was gratified with the ſight of an ample ſupply of water, from five wells.

Here the enemy deſiſting from the purſuit,

Mr. Thomas had time to direct his attention to the situation of his own troops. The sick and wounded were conducted to a place of safety, together with the hostages which had been received from the enemy on the commencement of the late negotiations; and having rested and refreshed his men, Mr. Thomas recommenced hostilities on the enemy's country, and, by a succession of exactions and fines, soon obtained money sufficient to defray his expences, and satisfy his troops for their arrears.

By this time, the rajah of Jypoor, sensible of the injury which his country would sustain by these depredations, once more sent persons to offer terms to Vavon Row, for the evacuation of his territories. The terms were accepted, a sum of money paid, and hostilities ceased.

On the conclusion of the transactions, Mr. Thomas determined to retaliate on the rajah of Beykaneer, and punish him for the aid which he had afforded the prince of Jypoor the preceding year.

To comprehend, however, the nature of this

expedition, it will be neceſſary in this place to recur to a geographical and ſtatiſtical ſketch of this remarkable country.

The province of Beykaneer is bounded on the north by the country of the Batties, weſt by the deſert, ſouth-weſt by Jeſſelmere, and ſouth by Joudpoor; ſouth-eaſt by Jypoor, and eaſt by the diſtrict of Hurrianah. It is one hundred and twenty coſs from north to ſouth, and from fifty to eighty from eaſt to weſt; but is broadeſt in the centre. The country is elevated; the ſoil a light brown ſand, from the nature of which rain is ſwallowed up as ſoon as fallen. This circumſtance renders neceſſary a recourſe to the conſtruction of wells in all parts of the country. Theſe, which are made of brick, are in general from one to two hundred feet in depth, though towards the Jeſſelmere frontier they extend to no leſs than three hundred feet. For the ordinary purpoſes of life, and domeſtic conſumption, each family is careful to provide a ciſtern for the reception of rain water; as a dearth of this precious article frequently compels the inhabitants, by whole families, to migrate to a more favourable ſoil.

With the exception of a few villages towards the eaſtern boundary, the cultivation of Beykaneer is precarious; bajerah, and other ſorts of Indian pulſe, being all that are produced. But horſes and bullocks are numerous. From the cauſes above ſtated, the inhabitants of Beykaneer are obliged in a great meaſure to depend upon their neighbours for the neceſſary ſupplies of proviſions; as even in the few places moſt favourable for cultivation the produce of the fields ſcarcely recompenſes the labour of the peaſant.

The city of Beykaneer is ſpacious, well-built, and ſurrounded by a wall of conker.

One mile ſouth-weſt of the city is the fort where the rajah reſides. It is a place of conſiderable ſtrength, built in the Indian ſtyle, and encompaſſed by a broad and deep ditch; but the chief ſecurity of both the city and fort is owing to the ſcarcity of water in the ſurrounding country.

The form of government in Beykaneer reſembles that of Joudpoor, for here alſo both the property and lives of the ſubject are entirely at the diſpoſal of the prince.

Soorut Sing, the preſent ruler of Beykaneer, has been of late years compelled to maintain an army of mercenaries for the ſecurity of his authority. For though at his acceſſion to the government he found himſelf poſſeſſed of a full treaſury, which the wiſdom and foreſight of his anceſtors had hoarded up with frugality and care; yet from boundleſs profuſion and thoughtleſs extravagance this was quickly diſſipated; and his neceſſities compelling him to have recourſe to extortions to ſupply his extravagance, he has, by becoming cruel, tyrannical, and oppreſſive, thereby alienated the love of his ſubjects.*

* In the year 1799, the rajah of Beykaneer committed an act deserving of the highest reprobation, and which stands confirmed on the authority of Mr. Thomas.

A party who were sent by Vizier Ali, the spurious nawaub of Oude, to the country of Zemaun Shah, were, by order of Soorut Sing, the present sovereign, not only detained prisoners in their passage through his territories, but plundered of their property and treasure to the amount of twenty-seven lacks of rupees, and finally put to death.

The inhabitants of Beykaneer are in general Rajpoots, and ſpring from the parent ſtock of Oudipore, as will be hereafter noticed in the hiſtorical ſketch of that remarkable country. This of courſe attaches to them a ſimilarity of habits and manners. It has however been remarked that although Rajpoots, and of the Rhatore tribe, the Beykaneerians are cruel in diſpoſition, cowardly, and treacherous. Theſe degenerate ſymptoms may be attributed partly to their indolent and inactive ſtate for a long period of years; and partly to a relaxation in their ancient ſimplicity of manners, occaſioned by the bad example ſet them by their own princes.

The revenues of Beykaneer amount to about three lacks of rupees; though the rajah has occaſionally found means, by laying duties and vexatious impoſts on the merchants paſſing through his country, to realize nearly double that ſum.

The trade formerly paſſing from the port of Soorat to Tatta on the Indus, entered from thence the Beykaneer province. The usual route of the caravans was through Joudpore and the province of Jesselmere; but the rapacity and injustice of the reigning prince, as above related, have, of late years, if not utterly annihilated commerce, at least directed its course into other channels: of this neglect the rajah of Jypore has reaped the principal benefit, by turning the most lucrative branches of commerce into his own territories.

The force of Beykaneer may amount on the whole to eight thousand men; two fifths of which are cavalry, and the remainder infantry and artillery. In the service of this prince are several Europeans of different nations, who reside within the fort of Beykaneer.

The rajah of Beykaneer has many enemies, the principal of which are his neighbours the Batties, whose country he invaded about nine years since, but without success. He has, in like manner, been unsuccessful in several attempts lately made in the district of Churoo.

Considering the nature of the soil and climate

of this country, it muſt appear matter of no ſmall ſurprize, that any people ſhould voluntarily have ſelected ſo barren and unprofitable a ſpot for a permanent reſidence. In Mr. Thomas's opinion, this determination muſt have originated in the predilection manifeſted by the firſt ſettlers for this dreary ſolitude; either from a romantic wiſh for retirement among themſelves, or occaſioned by the hatred which they entertained againſt the oppreſſion and injuſtice of their former rulers. The natives of this diſtrict are robuſt, hardy, and excellent farmers.

Adjoining the province of Beykaneer is the diſtrict called the Lacky Jungle, ſo much and ſo deſervedly celebrated for the fertility of its paſture lands, and for a breed of excellent horſes of the higheſt eſtimation in India. The Lacky Jungle is compriſed within the diſtrict of Batinda, forming a circle of about twenty-four coſſes of the country each way. On the north it is bounded by the country of Roy Kelaun, eaſt by the province of Hurrianah, ſouth by Batnier, and weſt by the great deſert.

It is ſituated twenty-two coſs north of Batnier, and fifty weſt of Pattialah, to whoſe chief the rajah is tributary.* The ſoil being ſandy, the wells are of conſiderable depth. The country yields rice and bajerah, and other ſorts of grain, but not in abundance. The chief excellency of the diſtrict conſiſts in its paſture lands, which for a ſucceſſion of ages have been celebrated as a nurſery for cattle. The original breed in this country has been much improved by Perſian horſes, which were introduced during the ſucceſſive invaſions of Nadir Shah and the Abdallis into Hindooſtan. This breed however has of late years been much neglected. This Mr. Thomas attributes to the exactions of the government, or rather to the rapacity of the miniſters of the rajah, who frequently compel the proprietors of the horſes to ſell them at their own price, much under the real value; and when purchaſed they are by theſe rapacious men ſent, on their own accounts, to different parts of the peninſula, and ſold at a conſiderable profit.

* Consult the map.—This part of the country however stands in need of an actual survey, which would be both curious and interesting.

This impolitic meaſure has not only cauſed a decreaſe in the preſent breed, but has alſo deterred the inhabitants from extending the traffic; though, on the contrary, if the breeders of the horſes were allowed a fair and equitable market, and they were to be exempted from thoſe vexatious drawbacks, the commerce might again flouriſh, and the proprietors of land in the Lacky Jungle and its vicinity would have a certain preference in ſupplying the neighbouring ſtates with plenty of the fineſt horſes in India.

The prices of the horſes are variable, and obtain according to the quality of the animal; they are in general from two hundred to one thouſand rupees in value, which latter ſum is ſeldom exceeded.

It is remarked that the breeders are averſe to diſpoſe of their brood mares; and if prevailed upon to do ſo, will exact double price: though in general with regard to foreigners, they cannot be perſuaded to part with a brood mare for any price.

While breeding, the mares and foals are kept apart from the horses. The women and children look after them during the day-time. At the season of the periodical rains they are allowed to graze, and are brought home at night; but in the cold and dry seasons they are fed upon hay, which is dried in the same manner as in Europe; a custom common throughout the west of India.

One thing only diminishes the excellence of this breed, which is a disease of the most distressing nature. A species of musquitoes, called by the natives Dunkh*, and sometimes Fetha, are not only very troublesome to the animals, by annoying them with their stings, but in a short time degenerating into an incurable cancer, the horses die.

This disorder prevails chiefly in the neigh-

* This is remarkable, and it would no doubt amply recompense the labour any gentleman of science might bestow in investigating the causes of this extraordinary distemper, and pointing out a remedy; more especially, as it seems peculiar to the district called the Lacky Jungle.

bourhood of the Cuggur river, more particularly about the towns of Futtiahbad, Seerſah, and Runyah; and it is computed that in theſe places, and the interior parts of the Lacky Jungle, the yearly loſs ſuſtained by the ravages of this pernicious inſect is eſtimated at one-fourth of the horſes* that are produced.

Returning from our geographical excurſion, we now reſume the thread of our narrative. When reſolved on the invaſion of Beykaneer, Mr. Thomas, with great precaution and foreſight, had prepared a number of water-bags for the uſe of his army; a meaſure which the ſcarcity of water in that country rendered indiſpenſably neceſſary.

With this aid, and a reinforcement of troops, he on the commencement of the rainy ſeaſon began his march. The rajah, who had received

* In addition to the foregoing it may be observed, that though the best horses are said to be produced within the boundaries of the Lacky Jungle, Mr. Thomas affirms that equally good horses may be procured many coss distant from thence; a circumstance which may possibly have confounded the real Jungle with some other place.

intimation of the intended attack, was prepared to repel it. Being in want of artillery, and knowing he could not ſtand againſt Mr. Thomas on the plain, he ſtationed large bodies of infantry in each of the frontier towns.

The firſt attack was made on the village of Jeitpore, in which were three thouſand men. Mr. Thomas reſolved on an immediate aſſault; and carried the place, though with the loſs of two hundred of his troops. The lives and property of the ſurvivors were then ranſomed for a ſum of money; and ſucceſsful in this firſt onſet, Mr. Thomas met with but little reſiſtance during the remainder of the campaign. Intimidated by theſe repeated defeats, the rajah's followers deſerted in crowds; a few Rajpoots alone remained faithful to his cauſe.

Under circumſtances ſo unfavorable, the rajah diſpatched a vakeel to Mr. Thomas, to requeſt a ceſſation from hoſtilities, and conſent to an adjuſtment of former differences. The rajah agreed to pay the ſum of two lacks of rupees, part of which was delivered on the ſpot; and for the remainder bills were given upon merchants in Jypore, the amount of which Mr. Thomas never received.

It has before been remarked that Luckwah and his colleague had been ſuperſeded in their command, and made priſoners. This circumſtance afforded Mr. Thomas an opportunity of regaining poſſeſſion of the diſtricts belonging to the deceaſed Appakandarow, and which, as above related, had been made over in form to Furnaveeſe. Mr. Thomas now poſſeſſed himſelf of the diſtricts in queſtion, with an intent to preſent them to Appa's heir; but Ambajee and Mr. Perron, who had been lately nominated to the chief command in Hindooſtan, hearing of his intentions, united in requeſting Mr. Thomas to abſtain from interfering in the affair. Conſulting with Vavon Row on the ſubject, he was adviſed by that chief to comply, and at length aſſented. In recompence for this conceſſion, the Marhattas gave him the pergunnah of Badhli, which he added to his other acquiſitions.

Mr. Thomas next marched to Jeind, a town on the frontiers of Hurrianah and Punjab, belonging to Baug Sing. This chief had, from Mr. Thomas's first entering the province, behaved towards him in a hostile manner, for which Mr. Thomas now determined to retaliate. On his arrival at Jeind, the capital of Baug Sing, he attempted to storm the place, but was driven back with the loss of four hundred men. Undismayed even at a check so unexpected, Mr. Thomas, having fortified his camp agreeably to his usual custom, formed the blockade of the place; by which means, there being three thousand persons within the town, he expected to compel them to a surrender. In this hope he was for the present disappointed. The sister of Sahib Sing, of Puttialah, a woman of a masculine and intrepid spirit, attended by a large force, arrived to succour the place: with her also came Bugheel Sing, and other chiefs of the Seiks. Mr. Thomas, without hesitation, attacked the last-mentioned party with so much spirit that he compelled them to retire: and following up his victory, drove them through their own camp; which, consisting of straw huts, he quickly destroyed by fire. They returned however to the attack, and their numbers increasing, they were permitted, by the ſhameful ſupineneſs of his own officers, to take poſſeſſion of two redoubts, by which many of his beſt men were cut to pieces. Supplies of proviſion coming in ſlowly, and the country people perceiving the untoward ſituation of affairs, now declared againſt him, and joined the enemy. This compelled Mr. Thomas, after a blockade of three months, to raiſe the ſiege, and return to Hanſi. The enemy, by this time increaſed to ten thouſand men, followed in his rear; and to add to his diſtreſs, the chief of Puttialah appeared at the ſame time with ſeveral pieces of heavy artillery. A retreat in theſe countries being always deemed equivalent to a defeat, the peaſantry who roſe on all ſides increaſed the difficulty in his progreſs. In hope of diverting the enemy's attention, Mr. Thomas gave out that he was going to Jypore; which lying far diſtant from their own country, he expected would induce them to relinquiſh their purſuit. In this he was unſucceſsful; but the enemy having repeatedly attacked him, and as often been repulſed, now of their own accord drew off, and directed their march towards Hanſi. Hoping to intercept him before he could reach that place, in their route they encamped at Narnound, a town twenty coſs to the northward of Hanſi. Here Mr. Thomas reſolved to attack them. For this purpoſe he marched all night, and arriving by daybreak in their camp, gave them a complete defeat. Their tents, baggage, the howdahs of their elephants, the bazar, with one thouſand ſaddles, and about two hundred horſes, fell into his hands; but his troops diſperſing on all ſides in ſearch of plunder, prevented his becoming maſter of their artillery and elephants.

From the inclemency of the ſeaſon, Mr. Thomas was now neceſſitated to return to the place where he had depoſited his heavy baggage; and the Seiks, in their late defeat, repaired to Jeind. On their arrival they were refuſed admittance into the place, by the ſiſter of Sahib Sing. This lady, who, as we have before ſeen, had on ſeveral occaſions exhibited a ſpirit ſuperior to what could have been expected from her ſex, and far more decided than her brother, now offered to take the field in perſon. But the Seik chieftains, aſhamed in being exceeded in ſpirit by a woman, returned to encounter

Mr. Thomas, whom they found encamped near a large town. They now came to a resolution to conquer, or perish in the attempt: but whilst deliberating on the mode of attack, their own camp was suddenly assaulted during the night by a numerous and daring banditti, who sounded their trumpets with such loud alarms that the Seiks, thinking the whole force of Mr. Thomas was at hand, abandoned their camp with precipitation. This circumstance, though it occasioned no real loss to the Seiks, had great effect on the minds of the country people, and lessened their ideas of Seik prowess. The Seiks were now as desirous of peace as they had before been determined on the continuance of hostilities; and it was at length agreed between the contending parties that each should remain in possession of their several districts, as they stood before the siege of Jeind. Excepting the Rajah of Pattialah, all the rest were well satisfied with the termination of hostilities. He alone refused to sign the treaty, although, in spite of his remonstrances, it was done by his more spirited sister. For this conduct the Seik chief ungenerously evinced his resentment, by detaining her a prisoner; but Mr. Thomas, deeming it his duty to interfere on this occaſion, by threats compelled him to releaſe her.

About this time Mr. Thomas was invited by Ambajee to unite their forces: for his aſſiſtance Mr. Thomas was to receive the monthly ſum of fifty thouſand rupees. Having at preſent no particular deſtination, he cloſed with the terms: and agreeably to the inſtructions of Ambajee, prepared to lead his army to Oudipoor to encounter Luckwa; who by this time, having regained his liberty, was aſſembled in great force. As the country of Oudipoor conſtitutes one of the principal ſtates of Rajepootana, and is on ſeveral accounts extremely intereſting, we ſhall hope for pardon in digreſſing a little from the thread of our narrative, and proceed to take a retroſpective ſketch of its geographical poſition, and internal reſources.

CHAPTER X.

Geographical deſcription of the country of Oudipoor or Mewar—its conſtitution—manners and cuſtoms of the inhabitants—military operations in the Oudipoor country—termination of the campaign.

THE dominions of Oudipoor are ſeventy coſs from north to ſouth, and fifty from eaſt to weſt.

They are bounded on the north by Ajmere and the principality of Kiſhenghur, on the north and weſt by Joudepoor, on the ſouth and eaſt by the province of Malwa, and the north-eaſt by Kotah and Boondy.

The lands throughout Oudipoor are poſſeſſed by the princes, and chief nobility, and are held as Jaeedâd. Theſe lands at preſent can yield an annual revenue of a crore of rupees:

it formerly produced a larger ſum, but the depredations committed by the Mahrattas ſince taking poſſeſſion of a great part of this country, have cauſed its reduction to the preſent ſtandard; and though the Mahrattas ſince their conqueſt have permitted the landholders abovementioned to retain their lands, yet by frequent exactions and vexatious mulcts, their value to the proprietors is conſiderably leſſened.

Moſt of the opulent towns in Mewar, which formerly acknowledged the authority of the Oudipoor family, are now in the hands of the Mahrattas.

The rajah is in a ſtate ſimilar to that of the emperor at Delhi; he is entirely guided by Mahratta councils, and dependant on them in a great meaſure for his ſubſiſtence: but in Mr. Thomas's opinion, they have not yet obtained the ſtrong holds in his country, and this prince, at preſent ſo inſignificant, may poſſibly at no diſtant period free himſelf from their uſurpations.

The country of Oudipoor is very productive; it yields sugar-cane, indigo, tobacco, wheat, rice, barley, and in short every thing to be found in other parts of India in the greatest abundance.

In Oudipoor are found iron-mines, excellent timber, and in one part of the country is produced sulphur.

The generality of cattle, however, are inferior in quality to those of the more western countries: horses only are numerous, and may be procured at a moderate price.

The produce of the neighbouring states being nearly the same as that of Oudipoor, the trade with them is not considerable, but a very extensive commerce from all parts of India was formerly carried on through the agency of the Ghosseins of Nathdora; this of late years, through the oppressive government of the Mahrattas, has been obstructed in its progress, almost to annihilation.

This country is uncommonly strong by nature. The city of Oudipoor, which is situated in an amphitheatre of hills, is guarded in the approach by a deep and dangerous defile, which admits of only a ſingle carriage paſſing at a time. So extenſive is the circuit protected by this paſs, that between four and five hundred villages are contained within its range; but Oudipoor, thus ſurrounded by hills, is very unhealthy, and peculiarly ſo during the ſeaſon of the periodical rains.

The wells in the neighbourhood of the city, though but a ſmall diſtance from the ſurface of the earth, are ſtrongly impregnated with the mineral qualities of the water that flows from the neighbouring hills, a principal cauſe of the inſalubrity of this climate.

The internal adminiſtration of Oudipoor is extremely ſingular, and therefore merits attention.

The whole power of the ſtate was formerly veſted in ſixteen principal chieftains, who were accuſtomed to reſide at court, with a ſtipulated number of followers. Theſe chiefs diſtinguiſhed by the name of the ſixteen omrahs, and conſtantly reſiding at the capital, under the immediate eye of the ſovereign, this circumſtance rendered it impoſſible for them to tranſact the buſineſs of their reſpective domains in perſon. To remedy this inconvenience, thirty-two inferior chiefs were nominated to aſſiſt them with their counſels: theſe were deſignated the thirty-two omrahs; and in order to aſſiſt the latter, in the ordinary detail of buſineſs in the interior diſtricts, ſixty-four inferior officers were appointed, who from their number are alſo called the ſixty-four omrahs. Theſe combined, preſent a ſyſtem not very diſſimilar to that of the feudal tenures of Europe, prior to the conſolidation of the French monarchy, under the emperor Charlemagne,* though that prince has been blamed by hiſtorians for dividing his kingdom among his children.

In the original deſign of this extraordinary conſtitution, it was intended that a gradation of authority ſhould be eſtabliſhed by the

* Consult the History of France, vol. I. p. 59, et seq. Author anonymous.

ſmaller number controlling the greater; ſo that the thirty-two chiefs were to be ſubſervient to the decrees of the council of ſixteen, and by a ſimilar and progreſſive ratio the reſolutions of the ſixty-four were to be controlled by thoſe of the thirty-two.

But, as might reaſonably have been expected, the chiefs, by a frequent abuſe of power, at length ſanctioned the interference of the prince; who by intrigues and ſowing diſſenſions among them, gradually recovered the exerciſe of his own authority.

He therefore forbade theſe high-ſpirited nobles to interfere with each others' concerns: and to remedy the inconveniences that government might ſuſtain from their private feuds, the rajah appointed of his own accord a dewaun, or controller-general; to whom all complaints from the omrahs or the ſubjects within their reſpective diſtricts were to be made, and whoſe adjudication was to be conſidered as final. As the lands throughout Oudipoor had formerly been divided among the omrahs, with a ſlight variation they have ſo continued to the present day; but the former authority and political consequence enjoyed by these omrahs in the administration of the government, have long ceased, and at present Mahratta influence alone prevails in the dominions of Oudipoor.

The policy of the Mahrattas has of late been directed to distress the people of Oudipoor with vexatious fines, rather than to dispossess them altogether, as they apprehend, if driven to desperation, the Rajepoots might not only unite in a common cause, but by deserting the level country and taking refuge in the mountains, render their complete subjection extremely difficult.

The nobility of Oudipoor are rajepoots of the tribe called Sesodia. This tribe among them is esteemed the purest and most noble; a few are Rahtours. In their persons the Oudipoor Rajepoots are not so comely as the neighbouring rahtours, nor are they so courageous, although they frequently intermarry with that tribe. This distinction in the rajepoot blood, in Mr. Thomas's opinion, may be traced to the unhealthineſs of the climate. Though affable in their manners and civil to ſtrangers, the rajepoots of Oudipoor do not poſſeſs an equal ſhare of ſincerity with their brethren in other parts of Rajepootana.

The military force of Oudipoor may be eſtimated at twelve thouſand cavalry; the infantry, which is retained by the different omrahs in their reſpective forts to guard againſt Mahratta invaſion, is very inconſiderable. The arms of the Oudipoor rajepoots conſiſt of a matchlock, a lance, and a ſabre, though the former are not ſo much uſed as the two latter.

They are fond of glittering armour; and clothe their horſes with a thick quilting, which it is ſaid will reſiſt the ſtroke of a ſabre.

Mr. Thomas moreover conſiders the inhabitants of Oudipoor as more inclined to pomp and luxury than the other tribes.

It is however to be remarked, that when the honour of their women is concerned, or they are afraid of their being inſulted, the Rajepoots of Oudipoor, in common with their brethren in the other ſtates, not only make a deſperate reſiſtance, but if unſucceſsful ſeldom ſurvive their diſgrace.

If the natural ſtrength of this country, its internal reſources, and, above all, the ſpirited and warlike character of its inhabitants, be conſidered with attention, it can ſurely, concludes Mr. Thomas, be no matter of wonder, that the ſubjugation of a country ſo difficult of acceſs ſhould be attended with innumerable obſtacles; or that the hardy and independant chiefs, immured within their native faſtneſſes, ſhould not only ſtill be enabled to preſerve themſelves from the Mahratta yoke, but continue even to the preſent hour to enjoy their patrimonial eſtates in an undiſturbed tranquillity.

We muſt now carry back our narrative to the commencement of Mr. Thomas's expedition againſt Luckwa; who, as before ſtated, had taken a ſtrong poſition on the frontiers of Oudipoor.

While on the march towards that country, Mr. Thomas was alarmed by a mutiny which broke out among his troops, occaſioned by delay in the payment of their arrears. As an apology for a conduct ſo unmilitary, they urged, that as they were now marching towards the Deccan*, their families who were left behind would ſuſtain much inconvenience. Although there appeared ſome reaſon for the demand, Mr. Thomas deeming it a dangerous precedent to yield compliance, therefore gave them a denial. The mutineers, growing outrageous, wiſhed to ſurround and take him priſoner: this he evaded by encamping apart from them with the ſoldiers who were ſtill faithful. He then called in a body of cavalry to his aſſiſtance, when the mutineers advanced with their guns to attack him. Reſolved to repreſs their inſolence or periſh in the attempt, Mr. Thomas now mounted his horſe, and went to meet them. Several ſhot were fired

* This word implies the south, in opposition to *ootur* or the north: *poorub* is the east, and *puchum* the west.

at him: but having resolutely seized on the ringleaders, he expelled them from the camp; and the remainder, perceiving the fate of their comrades, returned to their duty.

He then proceeded against Luckwa. On the road he was joined by vakeels from the rajahs of Joudpoor, Jypoor, and Kishen Ghur, each of whom brought presents from their respective masters. It was now represented to Mr. Thomas, that Scindiah having pardoned Luckwa, it was therefore improper to proceed to hostilities with that chief; but Mr. Thomas, who only consulted the interests of Ambajee in whose service he was now engaged, and from whom he had received positive orders to fight Luckwa wherever he came up with him, did not, from these considerations, think himself at liberty to desist. But the former mutiny among his troops, not having been properly quelled, from a mistaken lenity in Mr. Thomas, and unwillingness on his part to push matters to extremities, now broke out again with redoubled violence. With his usual prompitude, he seized on the ringleaders, and instantly caused one of them to be blown from the mouth of a cannon; the others were ſecured by putting them in irons: this prompt ſeverity was attended with the happieſt effect, the mutiny was entirely ſubdued, and was the laſt he ever experienced.

He was now joined by a brigade of troops under Mr. Sutherland, who came for the avowed purpoſe of oppoſing Luckwa. On uniting their force, they advanced towards Luckwa. That chief, as yet unable to make an effectual reſiſtance, encamped near the paſs leading to Oudipore, the nature of which has been before deſcribed. Into this paſs he threw his heavy baggage and ſtores, a meaſure which on any other occaſion would have proved his ruin; but Luckwa had previouſly received information that the rana of Oudipore, being favourably inclined towards him, was ready to afford protection to himſelf and followers.

A plan of attack was now concerted by Mr. Thomas and Mr. Sutherland, and the enſuing morning named for carrying it into execution. That very night, however, Mr. Sutherland, without aſſigning any cauſe, to Mr. Thomas's utter aſtoniſhment, thought proper to decamp, and leave him to conduct the operations againſt Luckwa with his own troops.

This circumſtance inſpired Luckwa with confidence; and he, who from the untoward ſituation of his affairs, had before been humble, now became haughty in proportion to their alteration. He ſent letters to the different chiefs in the neighbourhood, commanding them to join his ſtandard. Three days after Mr. Sutherland's retreat, Mr. Thomas, leaving Ambajee with his troops to protect the baggage, advanced againſt Luckwa in order of battle; but the action was at that time prevented by the coming on of a moſt tremendous ſtorm of rain, thunder, and lightning, which induced Luckwa to halt. Mr. Thomas's poſition being favourable for cavalry to act, of which the enemy's force chiefly conſiſted, and far ſuperior in number, he was deſirous of changing it; and accordingly, moving more to the left, he took poſt on a riſing ground from whence he could have nothing to apprehend from an attack of horſe. When the ſtorm was over, Luckwa again advanced towards Mr.

Thomas; but seeing his advantageous positition, and having lost a number of men in his approach from the fire of Mr. Thomas's artillery, he thought proper to draw off the field. Mr. Thomas, after a severe and fatiguing service during the day-time, returned in the evening to his own camp.

At midnight, vakeels from Luckwa arriving in the camp, produced letters from Scindiah, in which that chief repeated his commands for hostilities to cease on both sides, he having nominated Luckwa to the government of all his possessions north of the Nerbuddah. In the morning a council of war being held, the different sirdars each delivered his own opinion. Mr. Thomas, on his part, observed, that being employed by Ambajee for the express purpose of reducing the province of Mewar to his authority, he could consent to no terms in which the evacuation of that country by Luckwa was not a leading article.

After much negotiation, a proposal was made for both armies to march to the northern frontier, and there wait for fresh instructions from

Scindiah on the ſubject. Mr. Thomas, well appriſed of the inſincerity of Luckwa, knew that he only wiſhed to gain time, in order to form a junction with a body of troops now on their march to join him from Ajemere, and to get that country in his rear, which, as the fort and city of Ajemere belonged to him, would enable him to receive a conſtant ſupply of proviſions; for theſe reaſons, therefore, he was averſe to the propoſal. He knew alſo, that their preſent ſituation near Oudipore would be much benefited when the periodical rains, which were now daily expected, ſhould ſet in, as he would then be able to procure a ſupply of forage, of which they were in great want.

Theſe points he ſubmitted to Ambajee's conſideration, but in vain, for that chief's principal officers having been gained over by bribes, declined acting againſt Luckwa, until anſwers to the propoſitions referred to Scindia ſhould be received.

In thoſe reſolutions Mr. Thomas unwillingly acquieſced. The armies commenced their march, and although only at a diſtance of fifty coſs (the rains having overtaken them in their route) fifteen days had elapſed before they reached the northern frontier. Luckwa having by this time been reinforced by the troops which he expected, as alſo by ſome from Oudipoor, peremptorily refuſed to evacuate the country. He accordingly recommenced hoſtilities, and marched againſt Mr. Thomas. Ambajees's troops, who were encamped on an extenſive plain, were in conſequence open to attacks of cavalry; Mr. Thomas with his uſual prudence had taken poſt on the ſpot of ground ſurrounded on all ſides by nullahs and ravines. In a council of war held on the occaſion, it was determined that Ambajee's force ſhould encamp in Mr. Thomas's rear, by which means they would be ſecure from any attempt of the enemy's horſe. Prior to this determination of the council being known, a battalion who had began to dreſs their victuals, could not be perſuaded to move off until they had finiſhed their meal; the conſequence of this delay proved fatal; Luckwa, too late ſenſible of his error in not poſſeſſing himſelf of the ground occupied by Mr. Thomas, nevertheleſs attempted to take a redoubt that lay in his front; for this purpose he advanced with resolution, but being soon compelled to retreat, he directed his infantry to remain on the defensive; and eager to revenge his ill success, at the head of a strong detachment of cavalry, he fell suddenly upon the battalion before mentioned, who in their defenceless state were almost cut to pieces. Mr. Thomas, leaving two battalions to cover Ambajee, now proceeded with the remainder to the attack of Luckwa's main body, but a heavy shower of rain falling, and the sudden swelling of the nullahs, prevented further hostilities on that day. The rain continued without intermission for eight days, during which time no opportunity occurred of renewing the contest; frequent skirmishes however took place. It was customary for Luckwa and some of his principal Sirdars, attended by a select body of horse, to pay daily visits to Mr. Thomas: they usually posted themselves between the camp and the town of Shahpoora, from whence he received supplies of grain.

To deceive the enemy on this occasion, Mr. Thomas was accustomed to change the uniforms and colours of his own people; and having by feints got within shot of the enemy, he frequently opened a smart cannonade; one in particular, the enemy approaching so near, that Luckwa himself could be easily distinguished. Mr. Thomas, by a brisk and well-directed fire, compelled them to a speedy retreat, after a considerable loss in men and horses. These skirmishes, though harassing to the troops, did not occasion much loss to either party, who were now in daily expectation of receiving orders from Scindiah to desist from hostilities. Intelligence now arrived that Perron, taking advantage of Mr. Thomas's absence, had invaded the purgunnah of Jyjur, and was moreover committing depredations on other parts of his possessions. This intelligence he wished to keep secret, but Luckwa, who had previously received similar intimation, now made Mr. Thomas very handsome offers to induce him to join his standard, but these were resolutely rejected. Mr. Thomas moreover acquainted Luckwa, that though he might possibly leave the service of Ambajee at the termination of the present campaign, he could never become his enemy, nor connect himself with thoſe who were. This anſwer diſpleaſed Luckwa; he complained much in his durbar of Mr. Thomas, who he ſaid was a man of a moſt unaccountable character; that although repeated orders had been received from Scindiah to ceaſe hoſtilities, he could not be prevailed on to obey them; and finally charged him with nothing leſs than aiming at the expiration of Scindiah's authority, and the eſtabliſhment of his own.

Not content with the falſeneſs of theſe accuſations, Luckwa privately ſent emiſſaries into Mr. Thomas's camp to ſow diſſenſions among his troops, but they being diſcovered by his hircarrahs,* were ſeized, put into confinement, and there detained during the remainder of the campaign.

The arts uſed by Luckwa on this occaſion having failed, Mr. Thomas conciliated the good opinion of his ſoldiers, by an aſſurance of ſpeedily reconducting them to their own country. The force of Luckwa at this period

* Meſſengers.

amounted to nine thouſand cavalry, ſix thouſand regular infantry, two thouſand Rohillas, and about five or ſix thouſand mercenaries, together with ninety pieces of artillery.

Mr. Thomas had only ſix battalions, by deſertion much reduced, one hundred and fifty cavalry, three hundred Rohillas and twenty-two pieces of artillery.

With this force comparatively ſo ſmall, he was compelled not only to provide for the ſafety of Ambajee, but the ſecurity of the camp, to eſcort proviſions, and procure ſupplies of forage for the whole.

Several actions took place, in which Mr. Thomas was uſually ſucceſsful, having frequently driven his antagoniſt back to his camp. On one occaſion Luckwa narrowly eſcaped a total defeat: he drew out his whole army, and advanced upon Mr. Thomas, who, at the time having only two battalions, was compelled to retire; Luckwa followed in his rear to the ſkirts of his encampment, when, being ſuddenly joined by three additional battalions and a ſupply of ammunition, unexpectedly turning on his purſuers, gave them a moſt ſevere check.

Luckwa returned in confuſion with the loſs of a great many men; and ſo great was the conſternation, that the darkneſs of the night alone ſaved him from a total defeat. Between the camps there ran a nullah, the north ſide of which was occupied by the army of Luckwa; and the troops of Ambajee and Mr. Thomas were ſtationed on the ſouth. Ambajee, in order to prevent the advance of Luckwa's artillery, who endeavoured to open upon him, fortified an advanced redoubt on the north ſide of the nullah, but too far detached from his main body to receive ſuccour in caſe of an attack. For its defence, were ſtationed three battalions of ſepoys, ſix pieces of cannon, and one thouſand Ghoſſeins. To ſupport theſe, three battalions were poſted at a ſhort diſtance in the rear. A heavy rain had fell for twenty four hours, which cauſed two large reſervoirs to overflow their banks, by which means the nullah riſing to a great height, became impaſſable, and thereby intercepted the communication between the camps. Luckwa availed himſelf of this opportunity, and attacked the poſt before-mentioned with great vigour and reſolution; his men in advancing to the aſſault were up to their necks in water, which reſolute conduct infuſed ſuch terror into the men in the redoubt, that being panick ſtruck, they ſurrendered without firing a ſhot. The Ghoſſeins alone refuſed to ſubmit; and, after a brave though fruitleſs reſiſtance, were cut to pieces. Ambajee's troops, who before this diſaſter refuſed to fight, now deſerted in great numbers. Luckwa alſo had by his intrigues induced the Shahpoora Rajah to join in hoſtilities againſt Mr. Thomas, whoſe ſupplies by this means were entirely cut off. Although he had proviſions ſufficient for the conſumption of twenty days for his own troops, thoſe of Ambajee had not more than three. Should they be compelled to retreat unſupported by him, they would moſt likely be cut off by their active and vigilant enemy. Mr. Thomas was diſtreſſed for ammunition; his ſuperfluous ſtores having been left at Singanah, a place twenty coſs diſtant from their preſent encampment: the diſtance did not permit his ſending a ſmall force to eſcort the ſtores, and from preſent circumſtances he was unable to detach a larger party. For theſe reaſons, he thought it more adviſable to march himſelf, and having procured the neceſſary ſupplies, to return to his former ground; but Ambajee's ſick and wounded men having been left on the ground, Mr. Thomas, with his accuſtomed humanity, generouſly advanced money to procure them carriage to the place. In his retreat he was purſued by a party from Luckwa's army; but after ſeveral ineffectual attempts the enemy deſiſted, and he completed the remainder of his march unmoleſted. We have before had occaſion to remark that Ambajee was ſenſible of his ill conduct in authoriſing an attack on Mr. Thomas's poſſeſſions, who had ever ſerved him with fidelity; that chief now wrote letters excuſing theſe attacks, and laying the blame on the enmity of Mr. Perron.

In fact, both Ambajee and Perron, ſuppoſing that Luckwa had been compelled to evacuate the Mewar, concluded there was no further occaſion for Mr. Thomas's ſervices; the preſent time, therefore, appeared to them moſt ſavourable for ſeizing his country; but perceiving his reſolute conduct and ſteady adherence to their intereſts during the late conflict, they ultimately grew aſhamed of their proceedings, and deſiſted.

Mr. Thomas, though diſſatisfied at the treatment he had experienced, neverthele ſs reſolved, from prudential motives, to appear content; and the diſtricts which had been taken from him having been reſtored, the matter was finally dropped.

Arriving at Singana, he completed his ammunition and other requiſites, and immediately recommenced his march againſt Luckwa; that chief had inveſted a fort about thirty coſs to the north eaſt of Singanah. Advancing by ſlow and eaſy marches through the diſtricts occupied by Agagee Mirtha, Mr. Thomas thought proper to puniſh that chief for his conduct on a late occaſion, in having invited the country people to declare againſt him.

In a few days he arrived within twelve

miles of Luckwa's camp, which he intended to attack the next morning; but Luckwa, deeming himſelf unequal to the conteſt, ſuddenly decamped from the fort he was beſieging, and having quitted the boundary in diſpute, he in two marches reached his own diſtricts in the province of Ajemere.

Letters had lately been received from Dowlut Rao Scindiah, enjoining Mr. Thomas to obey Luckwa, and put an end to the conteſt. To theſe he had uniformly replied, that being in the ſervice of Ambajee, he could only pay obedience to the orders of that chief; and in this he was juſtified by expreſs and repeated commands not to ceaſe from hoſtilities until Luckwa had quitted the dominions of Oudipoore.

That object being now happily accompliſhed, Mr. Thomas employed himſelf in levying contributions to reimburſe Ambajee for the expences incurred during the campaign. He collected near four lacks of rupees, a ſum conſiderably beyond the actual expenditure, and could have raiſed a great deal more, had not Mr. Perron about this time broke the treaty into which he had lately entered with Ambajee.

This treaty ſtipulated, that ſhould Scindiah hereafter think proper to reinſtate Luckwa in his authority, they were to act in concert, a meaſure by which ſecurity in their reſpective poſſeſſions would be eſtabliſhed.

In this agreement it was alſo ſtipulated that Mewar ſhould remain in Ambajee's poſſeſſion. Mr. Perron, who now began to entertain a jealouſy againſt Ambajee, entered into a private and ſeparate treaty with Luckwa, whom he had gained over to his intereſt. The letters from Scindiah were produced, requeſting Ambajee to withdraw his troops from the Mewar, and put Luckwa in poſſeſſion of his country. Perron adviſed compliance with the order, and in caſe of refuſal threatened to aſſiſt Luckwa in taking poſſeſſion by force. In this ſtate of the buſineſs, Ambajee wrote letters to his collectors and to Mr. Thomas, ordering them to deliver over the country in diſpute, and withdraw the troops. Mr. Thomas, on receiving a cypher from Ambajee, complied.

Mr. Perron now marched to Jypore; Ambajee remained behind; and not long after the tranſaction above related, deſired Mr. Thomas to march to Duttiah. He was preparing to obey, when a contrary order arrived, deſiring him to join the united force of Ambajee and Luckwa. Mr. Thomas, from ſuch contradictory orders, ſuſpected treachery, and that Luckwa wiſhed only for this opportunity to effect his ruin.

Refuſing therefore compliance with the demand, he commenced his march northward.

Luckwa now throwing off the maſk, wiſhed to ſend a force after Mr. Thomas in order to puniſh him, but was not able to raiſe a ſupply of money ſufficient for the purpoſe. Mr. Thomas continued to levy contributions in the Ajemere province, through which he directed his march, and now confidered himfelf in a ftate of actual hoftility againft Luckwa.

His fituation had by this time become critical; the army of Luckwa was but twenty cofs to the eaftward of him; that of Jypore lay in his front; and Perron himfelf was endeavouring to hurt him at the court of the Rajah. The bad water of the mountainous country of Mewar having affected his army, a third part of the troops were fick, but Luckwa's troops were in a ftate of infubordination; and the Rajah of Jypore and Mr. Perron were at prefent overawed by the prefence of Colonel Collins, the Britifh Ambaffador at that court, who about the latter end of 1799 had arrived at Janaghur, to demand the delivery of the perfon of Vizier Alli, the fpurious Nawaub of Oude.

In this ftate of affairs, Mr. Thomas, after eluding every attempt to oppofe his progrefs, and having raifed contributions to the amount of two lacks of rupees, arrived in his own territory, defirous of obtaining fome repofe from the fatigues of his late perilous campaign.

His repoſe however on this occaſion was not of long duration; the force which he had left behind to collect the revenues having accompliſhed their purpoſe, now joined him; and finding himſelf at eaſe with regard to the Mahrattas, he reſolved to make an incurſion into the Punjaub, in order to puniſh Sahib Sing of Puttialah, who had undeſervedly ill treated his ſiſter for entering into the negotiations with Mr. Thomas the preceding year. That chief had, moreover, during Mr. Thomas's abſence in the Mewar country, authoriſed depredations among his diſtricts; but hoſtilities were for the preſent prevented by the Seik chief agreeing to ſurrender certain villages, and paying a ſum of money as a compenſation for thoſe depredations.

Mr. Thomas next turned his arms againſt the Rajah of Beykaneer, who, as we have before had occaſion to remark, on the termination of his late diſpute, had given him falſe bills on the merchants of Jypore. That Prince had lately obtained ſome advantages over his neighbours the Battees, an extraordinary race with whom he had long been at variance, and whose country, from its singularity of situation, as well geographical as statistical, merits a digression from the ordinary course of Mr. Thomas's narrative.

CHAPTER XI.

Deſcriptive account of the country of the Batties —ſingular manners and cuſtoms of the inhabitants—military operations againſt the Rajah of Beykaneer—Mr. Thomas returns to Jyjûr.

THE country of the Batties is bounded on the north by the Punjab and the river Sutledge, eaſt by the diſtrict of Hurrianah, weſt by the deſert, and ſouth by Beykaneer.

It is fifty coſs from eaſt to weſt, and about one hundred from north to ſouth.

That part of the country beſt adapted for the purpoſes of cultivation is along the banks of the river Cuggur, extending from the town of Futtahbad to that of Batnier. The ſoil is uncommonly productive, which ariſes in a great meaſure from the immenſe body of water deſcending from the mountains during the rainy ſeáſon; this cauſing the banks of the river to overflow to an extent of ſeveral miles, leaves on the retiring of the waters a loamy earth, which rewards the labours of the peaſant in the produce of an abundant harveſt.

Where the river overflows, wheat, rice, and barley are plentiful, and in the higher parts of the country are likewiſe to be found thoſe different ſpecies of grain which are common throughout India. The remainder of the Battie country, owing to a ſcarcity of water, is unproductive.

The courſe of the Cuggur river has already been laid down in our detail of the Punjab. It is here, therefore, ſufficient to remark that during Mr. Thomas's reſidence at Batnier, he could perceive little veſtige of what was called the ancient bed of this river; but from the ſcanty information he procured, it appeared to him that the river, though it formerly ran along the north ſide of the fort, its channel had been choked up by vaſt quantities of earth forced down from the mountains; and, according to the prevailing opinion of the natives, though now loſt in the ſands weſt of the city, it formerly extended as far as the Sutledge, which it joined in the vicinity of Ferozepore.*

Batnier, the capital of the diſtrict, and reſidence of the Rajah, is two hundred miles weſt of Delhi, and about forty ſouth of Batinda. The towns of Arroah, Futtahbad, Sirſah, and Ranyah, conſtitute the other places of note in the Battie country; theſe towns, together with the numerous villages, afford a population ſufficient to bring into the field an army of twenty thouſand men, without detriment to the cultivation of the lands. Of late years, however, many of the Batties, migrating from their native country, have fixed their reſidence in the weſtern parts of the dominions of Oude, and at the preſent day ſeveral families of this ſingular tribe are to be met with in the vicinity of Chandowſy, in Rohilcund.

As peculiarity in manners more diſtinctly ſerves to diſcriminate the genius and character of a people, a few of the ſingularities obſerv-

* Consult the map.

able among the Batties may perhaps not be deemed unworthy of our notice. A desert separates them from any communication with the countries to the westward; parties are often formed for crossing this desert, in order to invade the nearest district. They set out numerous and well equipped; intelligent persons amongst them are selected by the rest as guides to the party, to whose orders, during the journey, they pay the most implicit obedience, and on arrival at the frontier of the enemy's country their authority is at an end.

For the performance of these journeys, they have camels, which are loaded with bread, water, and other necessary articles of provisions. This stock being previously sent off, is deposited at different parts of the desert, which extends from sixty to seventy coss. These places are considered as points of rendezvous to meet with their supplies; not a drop of water, or provisions of any kind, being otherwise procurable; and should these supplies fail by any accident, inevitable death awaits them all.

The guides, whom we have before mentioned, become ſkilful by long experience and conſtant practice. Without the aid of a tree, or land mark of any deſcription, to direct them in their march over this dreary deſert, they ſeldom fail not only to aſcertain the place where the proviſions are depoſited, but likewiſe to conduct the intrepid adventurers to the deſtined ſpot. It frequently happens, moreover, that individuals of the party, who, from heedleſsneſs and inattention, ſtray from the caravan, oppreſſed by the multiplied evils of thirſt, hunger, and fatigue, periſh miſerably in the deſert.

"So where our wide Numidian wastes extend,
"Sudden th' impetuous hurricanes descend,
"Wheel through the air, in circling eddies play,
"Tear up the sands, and sweep whole plains away.
"The helpless traveller with wild surprise,
"Sees the dry desert all around him rise,
"And, smother'd in the dusty whirlwind, dies !"*

In their progreſs during this ſingular march, the guides are directed by the Sun by day, and the North Star by night; and with theſe unerring marks they are enabled to perform journeys which appear almoſt incredible.

* See Addison's Cato.

These journeys are moreover performed with accuracy and exactness. Departing at night from a fixed or given point, and often steering different courses, by the aid of the signs abovementioned, they will, after a march of thirty, forty. and even fifty coss, return to the spot from whence they sat out, and, with the exception of rain or cloudy weather, scarce ever deviate from their point of destination. Should they be pressed for provisions on their journey, or have consumed their ordinary stock, a bullock or calf, belonging to the party, is killed, roasted, divided, and eaten on the spot; and at the conclusion of this primitive meal, the company resume the journey with their accustomed alacrity.*

We have hitherto seen the fairest side of the character of this extraordinary people. Candour requires us to state that they are cruel in their nature, savage and ferocious in the highest degree; that they have an utter abhorrence

* Are not these traits the Scythian characteristics? and do we not in the foregoing description recognise the pastoral lives of the Nomades of antiquity?

of all the usages of civilized life, are thieves from their birth, and scruple not, in their predatory incursions into the neighbouring districts, though unresisted, to add murder to robbery.

This thievish spirit may be said to have reached even the throne itself, as the Rajah has not been ashamed to declare, in Mr. Thomas's hearing, that he willingly participated in the spoils thus collected by his own subjects. This fact was ascertained by Mr. Thomas from the Rajah himself, during a residence of two months in his camp: in other respects, a good and humane character. The Rajah spoke without the least appearance of shame of the depredations committed by his subjects. When it was remarked that the soil and climate of his country were sufficiently fertile to supply the wants of the inhabitants by the honest labours of the plough, he replied, that the small number of Rajpoots in his service, compared with the mass of the country people, did not allow him to restrain the latter in those unlawful acts, as any interference with so old and established a custom would, in all probability, prove subversive of his own authority.

A people so enterprising must, no doubt, appear formidable to their enemies; yet if their utter contempt of subordination, and the weakness of their means of defence be duly considered; that they are a tumultuous rabble, void of order and discipline, it is matter of wonder that some of the neighbouring nations have not taken advantage of their weakness, and prevented this nest of banditti from interrupting their tranquillity. In their wars, or rather their depredations with the adjoining countries, they have been in general successful, and the territories of Sahib Sing, Loll Sing, and Baug Sing, chiefs of eminence among the Seiks, have frequently suffered by the inroads of this daring people, and been moreover not unfrequently compelled to purchase peace.

To these may likewise be added the country of the Balooches, west of the Sutledge; the district of Hurrianah; and the province of Beykaneer; all which have in turn sustained their ravages, and by which means, more than two thousand villages, which were once populous, highly cultivated, and produced a revenue of from twenty to thirty lacks of rupees, have now become a barren waste.

Another trait in the character of the Batties is their permitting their women to appear in public unveiled, and without any species of concealment, though common in other parts of India. On the contrary, with the exception of the wives of their chiefs, who are in general Rajpoots, the females are universally admitted to move about in company with the men, tending their flocks and herds, and, like the Scythians of old, traversing from place to place in search of forage and water.

"At th' approach of night,
"On the first friendly bank he throws him down,
"Or rests his head upon a rock till morn,
"Then rises fresh, pursues his wonted game;
"And if the following day he chance to find
"A new repast, or an untasted spring,
"Blesses his stars, and thinks it luxury.*

* See Addison's Cato.

The Batties are of the Mahomedan religion. In common with other Muſſulmans, they are fond of tobacco to exceſs; and whether on horſeback in the field, at the plough, or in their domeſtic avocations, are never ſeen without the hookha.

It has been remarked that this people can bring into the field from twenty to thirty thouſand men, but they are ill-armed, and without diſcipline.

The revenues of the Battie Prince ariſe chiefly from the plunder acquired by the incurſions of his ſubjects into the neighbouring ſtates, though it is difficult to aſcertain the exact receipts, but they do not in general amount to more than ten lacks of rupees.

The trade of the Batties is very circumſcribed, with the exception of the ſale of their ſurplus grain, ghee, and cattle of different kinds: they have little interference with other ſtates, and that chiefly with the petty merchants of Nohur and Behadra already mentioned, and with whom alone they hold a correſpondence from motives of religious veneration to the memory of Shaick Fereed, an eminent Mahomedan ſaint, who flouriſhed about the eighth century of the Hijerah.

This veneration is carried ſo far as to claim protection in his name. Though deaf to the voice of mercy in other reſpects, and cruel from their natural diſpoſition, yet in this inſtance the Batties reſtrain themſelves with a moderation truly ſingular.

Such is repreſented by Mr. Thomas to be a faithful portrait of the mixed character of this extraordinary people; and if the leading features of it be conſidered attentively by a reflecting obſerver, a compariſon with their barbariſm, and the happy reſult ariſing from the advantages of civiliſed life in other parts of the world, may be made to advantage, though it ſtill affords an impreſſive leſſon of the mutability of human nature, and the caprice and inſtability of all human inſtitutions.

The chiefs of the Batties were originally Rajpoots, but are now Mahomedans. About ſix hundred years ago their anceſtors migrated from the province of Jeſſelmere; and after ſeveral viciſſitudes of fortune, at length ſettled as cultivators of the ſoil in the diſtrict at preſent called the Battie country.

The majority of the preſent inhabitants, who acknowledge the authority of the deſcendants of the chiefs aforementioned, were originally Jauts, inhabiting the weſtern banks of the Sutledge, in the 29th degree of north latitude. They embraced the Mahomedan religion, and about one hundred years ſince were invited by the anceſtors of the preſent rajah to croſs the Sutledge, and ſettle in the vicinity of Batnier, where their deſcendants ſtill continue to reſide.

Reſuming our narration, after this digreſſion, it muſt now be remarked, that the local advantages poſſeſſed by the rajah of Beykaneer had induced him to erect a fort ſix coſs to the ſouth-weſt of Batinda, the capital of the Battee tribe, which ſerved in ſome meaſure to overawe thoſe deſperate marauders, or at leaſt to check their predatory incurſions into his own country. In this fort, exclusive of the garrison, he stationed a large body of cavalry, who so annoyed the Batties by frequent sallies, in which they took such numbers of cattle, that the inhabitants entertained thoughts of emigrating from their own country altogether.

When Mr. Thomas reached the frontiers of Beykaneer, the chiefs of the Batties, hearing of his arrival, were desirous of entering into a treaty with him; and, in order to secure him in their interests, offered the sum of 40,000 rupees, if he would reduce the fort abovementioned, and liberate them from their unpleasant situation.

The offer being accepted, after a march of ten days, Mr. Thomas reached the city of Batnier, the most western habitation in that part of India.*

This city, occupied by the troops of Bey-

* In this sense at least it is understood at present, there being no habitation west of it until you pass the Sutledge, from whence commences the country of the Balooches, who are at present tributaries to Zemaun Shah, king of Cabul.—Consult the map.

kaneer, was, from its natural position, almost inaccessible to an enemy, there being no water to be procured nearer than twelve miles. The garrison being numerous, Mr. Thomas thought it most eligible to batter in breach, which he did, and was making the necessary preparations for storming, when the enemy capitulated. He allowed them to march out with the honours of war, and immediately put the Battie chiefs in possession of the place.

Several other places were then taken possession of, and various actions took place, by which, and the unhealthiness of the climate, Mr. Thomas's troops were reduced to one third only of their original strength. This was the more unpleasant, as the brother of one of the chiefs abovementioned, who was at variance with him, commenced hostilities against Mr. Thomas, who, on account of the deficiency of his force, from the causes above stated, being scarcely equal to the encounter, was compelled to fortify his camp.

By night the enemy made frequent attacks; but, unsuccessful in all attempts, at length gave up the point, and withdrew their army.

Mr. Thomas then marched and took poſſeſſion of the town of Futtahbad, which with ſeveral others he burnt, and would now, in all probability, have got poſſeſſion of the whole country, had not the enemy at this time received aſſiſtance from their neighbour, the Seik chief of Puttialah. That chief, having ſent one thouſand cavalry to their aid, and concluded a treaty of alliance, Mr. Thomas did not deem the preſent moment favourable for a proſecution of hoſtilities. He therefore returned to Jyjur, in order to afford ſome relief to his people from the diſtempers they had contracted in the courſe of the campaign.

About this time, Luckwa, through the intrigues of Mr. Perron at Scindiah's durbar, had been again ſuperſeded in his command. To haſten his downfall, and if poſſible take him priſoner, Perron marched againſt him with his whole force.

But Luckwa, leaving his camp and baggage a prey to the enemy (who on their arrival were too much taken up in plundering to follow in the purſuit), and having previouſly ſent off his family to ſeek an aſylum in the dominions of Joudpore, thus effected his own eſcape.

Among the Rajpoot ſtates, the ſituation of Joudpore is deſerving of particular attention; and we ſhall therefore, as on ſimilar occaſions, turning aſide from the detail of military tranſactions, embrace the opportunity thus afforded of taking a retroſpective ſketch of the reſources of the country, as well as preſent our readers with an account of ſome of the manners and cuſtoms peculiar to this ſingular people.

CHAPTER XII.

Geographical deſcription of Joudpoor or Marwar —Manners and cuſtoms of the inhabitants— —Hiſtory—Mr. Thomas's military operations —Capture of Bhaut—Tranſactions in the territories of Roy Kellaun.

JOUDPOOR or Marwar is bounded on the north by Beykaneer, north-weſt by Jeſſelmere, and weſt by the deſert; on the ſouth-weſt by the country of the Sindys, ſouth by the province of Guzurat, ſouth-eaſt by Mewar, and eaſt by the dominions of Jypoor.

It is in length two hundred and twenty coſs, and in breadth one hundred and eighty, at the computation of two Britiſh miles to the coſs.

This extent of country is ſuppoſed formerly to have contained from eight to ten thouſand villages, including the capital towns within its range. The population was then great, but at preſent it poſſeſſes not more than five thouſand inhabited villages, with a conſiderable decreaſe of population. The ſouthern, ſouth-eaſtern, and eaſtern frontiers of Joudpoor are abundantly fertile. The land is well watered by ſtreams, which, as in Mewar, flow from the mountains. It yields wheat, barley, and other kinds of grain common in India. Excluſive of theſe advantages, lead mines are found, which conſiderably add to the revenues of the ſtate. The imports into Joudpoor conſiſt of cloths, ſhawls, ſpices, opium, rice, ſugar, ſteel, and iron. They export ſalt, camels, bullocks, and horſes: the latter are ſtrong, boney, and of high ſtature. The bullocks are of a very large ſize, as are likewiſe the camels. In ſhort, the breed of cattle in general is ſuperior to that of the neighbouring ſtates.

The inhabitants of Joudpoor are Rhatore Rajepoots. They are not only a more comely race of men as to perſon, but are braver, poſſeſs a higher ſenſe of honour, and are more independant than their ſurrounding neighbours. Mr. Thomas aſcribes theſe diſtinguiſhing characteriſtics to phyſical cauſes, to the influence of climate, and to their intermarrying with the pureſt caſt of the Rajepoot tribes. Theſe are the Seeſodyah, the Kutchwah, the Adda, and the Bawtee. To theſe cauſes may be added the good examples ſet them, both as to manners and morals, by a ſucceſſion of wiſe and prudent princes, who, firſt by their achievements in war abroad, and afterwards by the care they took of their affairs at home, in the internal regulations of their country, have contributed in a very high degree to ameliorate the character and diſpoſitions of their ſubjects.

The Rhatore Rajepoots are mild in their manners, and are poſſeſſed of a natural politeneſs which renders their ſociety extremely agreeable. When a Rhatore has paſſed his word for protection, it may ſtrictly be relied on. They are averſe to litigious controverſy. In their ſocial converſations they carefully avoid diſputes, and pay the greateſt attention to the perſon who is ſpeaking. In their hoſpitality they exceed the bounds of more civiliſed nations: for ſo attentive are they to the performance of this duty, that, in the interior parts of the country, the head of a village will not ſit down to eat his own meal until he has been ſatisfied that travellers and ſtrangers have received every accommodation which his village affords. A rare and ſingular inſtance of primeval ſimplicity of manners!

They delight in warlike exerciſe, are fond of the chaſe, and firing their matchlocks. Retired after the fatigues of hunting, they are accuſtomed to hold ſocial aſſemblies. They liſten with great earneſtneſs and eagerneſs to the *bauhtee*, or poets, who, like the bards of of old, recite in heroic numbers the warlike deeds of their anceſtors.

In the adminiſtration of juſtice they are alike ſingular. Murder, the fouleſt of crimes, is ſeldom puniſhed with death; and for this reaſon, that it ſcarcely ever occurs, except when occaſioned by a ſpirit of revenge for perſonal injuries: and for this they have the ſanction of cuſtom from time immemorial.

Theft is puniſhed by baniſhment; ſmaller crimes by a reprimand, which, from the ſpirit of the Rhatore Rajepoot, generally terminates on a voluntary exile from his native country, where he cannot endure to live after being ſubjected to reproach. In this, likewiſe, the ſpirit of this extraordinary race is conſpicuous: a man who goes into voluntary exile may if he pleaſes, after a ſtated period, return to his native place; whereas the poſſibility of return is rigidly precluded to him who is baniſhed for the degrading vice of theft. Although the Rajepoot chiefs, in their reſpective diſtricts, aſſume to themſelves an excluſive and arbitrary right over the lives and property of their ſubjects, yet it is not conſidered by the natives as a hardſhip, as their mild, conciliating ſway renders eaſy the condition of the peaſantry.

Fugitives of all deſcriptions from the neighbouring countries are received without diſtinction; and, except in caſes of theft and murder, are ſure of protection and ſupport. So high a ſenſe do they entertain of the laws and rights of hoſpitality, that they not only refuſe to deliver up the delinquents, but are even accuſtomed to aſſiſt in forwarding them through the country to the confines of the neighbouring ſtate.

It does not appear that a cuſtom ſo ſingular obtains in any other part of Hindooſtan. In the management of their domeſtic concerns, the Rhatore Rajepoots are no leſs remarkable for their attention to the female part of the family.

A plurality of wives, though admitted by the laws of the country, is ſeldom practiſed, except among the princes and great men, who on theſe occaſions are actuated by motives of policy and ambition. Among this tribe of Rajepoots, the mother of the eldeſt ſon is held in moſt reſpect.

Females, on the death of their huſbands, often reſign themſelves to the flames with the moſt heroic fortitude.

This act is however voluntary. But, in the opinion of the Rajepoots themſelves, thoſe females would be diſhonoured in the eſtimation of their countrywomen who preferred dragging on a reproachful exiſtence. They would be ſhunned in ſociety; and at the houſe of their father, or that of their father-in-law, generally be compelled to paſs the remainder of their lives in ſolitary widowhood.

From the early period of ſix years of age, all Rajepoot females are concealed from the ſight and converſation of men, except their neareſt relations. In the table of conſanguinity on this occaſion are included fathers, uncles, brothers, and couſins.

With theſe exceptions, a Rajepoot lady would conſider her reputation as ſullied by expoſure to the ſight of a man. To ſo high a pitch indeed do they carry their proud ſenſe of honour in regard to the female character, that it not unfrequently terminates in a manner moſt ferocious and lamentable.

When an honourable Rajepoot, whoſe family is with him, finds himſelf ſurrounded by the enemy, and a force ſo ſuperior that the hope or poſſibility of eſcape is utterly excluded, he firſt enquires whether, if by ſurrender, he can ſecure the honour of his family. Should this be found impracticable, or even doubtful, he forms and immediately executes his deſperate project. Clothing himſelf in a yellow dreſs, which is the ſymbol of deſpair, he, in company with others of his neareſt relations, repairs to the apartments of the women, when the whole of the females are involved in a promiſcuous and indiſcriminate ſlaughter; the women themſelves, on this occaſion, not unfrequently raiſing their hands againſt their own lives!

On the completion of this horrid deed, the furious Rajepoot, ruſhing out like a lion, bears down every thing before him: it is death alone that can ſatisfy him for the loſs of his tendereſt and deareſt connections. In this inſtance alone will he ſtrike a falling foe. The act which he has lately committed works him up to a ſtate of abſolute inſanity. Deſpair gives him courage more than mortal; and if, by his enthuſiaſtic and furious onſet, he ſhould chance to overcome the enemy, though ever ſo ſuperior in point of numbers, when oppoſition is abſolutely at an end, and his frame exhauſted with fatigue, is on the point of yielding to nature, he diſdains to ſurvive the loſs of his family, but terminates the awful ſcene by generouſly plunging his ſword into his own boſom!

For theſe and other obſtinate prejudices, the Rajepoots have been accuſed of cruelty; but it muſt be conſidered, in extenuation of the act, that this reſolution is founded on principle; it is imbibed in their infancy, and almoſt ſucked in with their parent food; that it is juſtified by cuſtom and precedent, and that a Rajepoot who ſhould ſurvive the diſhonour of his wife and family, would be treated by his brethren to the remainder of his life with contempt and never-ending reproach.

Although the circumſtances above related do ſometimes occur, it is by no means frequent, ſince the ſpirit of this people being known, it is not difficult to be avoided.

Throughout Hindooſtan the ſanctity of the haram is in general reſpected; and, except in caſes of reſiſtance, hoſtility is ſeldom carried to extremity; while on the contrary it not unfrequently happens that, by a previous ſtipulation between the contending parties, the females of either family are accuſtomed to aſk and to receive the protection of their enemies.

The Rhatores intermarry with other tribes, but of the pureſt blood, though they will not give their children either to the Bundeelahs, Scindiahs, or Holkars, whom they conſider of inferior caſt and impure blood.

The cuſtom of putting to death the females of the family, as remarked on a former occaſion, likewiſe obtains among the Rhatore Rajepoots; although one of their late princes, rajah Beejah Sing, by prohibiting the ſhedding of blood of any kind throughout his dominions, endeavoured to reclaim them from this ſanguinary prejudice; the preſent ſovereign of Joudpoor, by name Becun Sing, being a weak prince, effeminate, and luxurious, his ſubjects have already relapſed into their ancient and moſt abhorred cuſtom. The chief force of Joudpoor is in cavalry, and has always been conſidered as formidable.

Their horſes are good; and their ſtrength in cavalry Mr. Thomas computes at twenty-five thouſand men; though, ſince the acceſſion of the late rajah, and in their wars with the Mahrattas, they have ſeldom been able to bring into the field more than twenty thousand Rhatore Rajepoots.

The rajah of Joudpoor has generally in his pay from four to six thousand mercenaries, two thousand of which are cavalry; and in cases of emergency he might expect to be joined by the troops of Beykaneer. His force in cavalry may on the whole be estimated at thirty thousand men.

On their infantry, like many others in the interior parts of India, they place but small reliance, being seldom employed except in the garrisons.

The artillery is numerous, and consists of several hundred pieces of cannon, most of which were taken by the ancestors of the present rajah, when that prince surprised the camp of the emperor Aurung Zebe, in the defiles of the Rhatore mountains, on the return of the imperial army from the Deccan.*

* Consult Dow's History of Hindoostan, vol. iii.

This artillery however, ſeveral of the pieces being ſo much honeycombed from age, and almoſt all of them deſtitute of carriages, cannot excite much apprehenſion. The arms of a Rhatore Rajepoot conſiſts of a ſcimitar, made of a ſpecies of iron called *ſarohee*, which, though well calculated for cutting, is brittle in ſubſtance; a ſpear, and ſome of them have matchlocks, though in general the Rhatores truſt to their ſwords.

Of their bravery we have before ſpoken; but their ſingularity of character extends even to their method in fighting, as they will not kill a flying enemy, or ſhed blood when reſiſtance ceaſes.

Averſe to plunder, though even in the enemy's country, they will not indulge themſelves in predatory warfare; a practice ſo common with the Mahrattas and other of their neighbours. It is in actual combat alone they are truly formidable. In the charge of cavalry in particular, Mr. Thomas thinks they are ſuperior to moſt of the horſemen in India; but when headed by their prince in perſon, or by a favourite and ſucceſsful general, they are in his opinion irreſiſtible.

The revenues of Joudpoor chiefly ariſe from the *rah darees*, or road-duties. There is likewiſe a duty levied on merchandiſe of all kinds, the excluſive revenue produced from the poll-tax in capital cities, which is conſidered as a kind of privy purſe to ſupply the expences of the ſovereign, and a ſtipulated annual tribute from thoſe chiefs who hold their lands in Jaiedad, for the payment of the troops.

Theſe together may amount to about twenty lacks of rupees, which is the ſole property of the rajah. With regard to other funds, eſpecially the tribute which is paid to the Mahrattas, the extra expences incurred by government in raiſing additional troops in times of emergency, and various other contingencies, theſe are ſubſcribed for by the principal landholders; and the money thus conſolidated is thrown into the general treaſury of the ſtate.

The Rhatore Rajepoots attribute their origin

and firſt ſettlement in Joudpoor to the following tradition, as handed down in regular ſucceſſion from father to ſon.

About ſeven hundred years ſince, three brothers of a noble family at Kinnouge quitted that city by mutual agreement, and travelled weſtward towards Jeſſelmere.

Their names were Joud Sing, Kundal Sing, and another whoſe name Mr. Thomas has forgotten.

In their route to the place above-mentioned they paſſed by the town of Joudpoor, at that time an inconſiderable place, inhabited by Bramins; who, happening to be at variance with their neighbours, ſolicited and obtained the aſſiſtance of the three brothers, and were, in conſequence, ſoon put in poſſeſſion of their rights. On the performance of this ſervice, the Bramins would gladly have got rid of their powerful allies; but they liking the country were deſirous of ſettling in it altogether, and for this purpoſe they ſent for their reſpective families, who had been left at Kinnouge.

The Bramins, however, at firſt reſiſted this intruſion, but in the end being detected in a conſpiracy to aſſaſſinate the Rajepoot chiefs, they fell a ſacrifice to their own treachery, and were themſelves, without mercy, put to the ſword.

From that period the authority of the Rajepoots commenced in Joudpoor, and Joud Sing, as the elder brother, gave his own name to the place where they had firſt ſtopped. He founded the preſent city of that name, which in proceſs of time became the capital of the Rhatore Rajepoots.

Kundul Sing, the ſecond brother, took poſſeſſion of the neighbouring territory of Beykaneer, where he ſettled with his family : and the deſcendants of the third brother at preſent occupy the diſtrict of Behadra.

Mr. Thomas not chooſing to remain inactive, and arrears to a large amount being due to him from his northern diſtricts, he reſolved to march thither. In his route he puniſhed a numerous and daring banditti, who had frequently annoyed him by their predatory attacks; and who, having been joined by numbers of the peasantry who were assembled in considerable force at the village of Seesana, now confident in their numbers, issued forth from their strong hold to give battle to Mr. Thomas on the plain. But their temerity proved their destruction; for his troops, after a desperate conflict, not only completely defeated the enemy by driving them off the plain, but followed so close at their heels as to enter the town along with the fugitives, where they killed and wounded upwards of seven hundred men. His own loss on this occasion was considerable; but the capture of this place struck such terror throughout the country, that the remainder submitted without a struggle.

Mr. Thomas having raised the necessary contributions, and being satisfied in regard to the arrears due to his troops, next levied contributions on the districts held by Simbonauth, one of Luckwa's collectors in the neighbourhood of Sehaurunpore. Simbonauth was at that time in the Doo Ab, with a numerous though confused and disorderly rabble. He had lately sustained some smart skirmishes with the troops ſent againſt him by Mr. Perron; but his troop having been corrupted by means of a large ſum of money, which Perron found means to diſtribute, Simbonauth was at length neceſſitated to ſubmit, and give up part of his diſtricts, to ſecure the remainder from the graſp of the Mahrattas.

Mr. Thomas having thus raiſed the ſum required, returned to Hanſi. About this time Mr. Perron, who had in vain exerted himſelf to obtain poſſeſſion of the perſon of Luckwa, or his family, returned from the army. Well aware that little was to be gained by open hoſtilities with the Rajepoots, he marched back to Delhi, "in order," ſays Mr. Thomas, "to "gather eaſier laurels from the grain merchant, "Simbonauth who was by this time once "more ready to attempt the recovery of the "diſtricts which he had been ſo recently com-"pelled to reſign."

Soon after his arrival at Delhi, Mr. Perron with a conſiderable body of men, having croſſed the Jumna, paſſed into the Dooab, to act againſt Simbonauth; at the ſame time he diſpatched letters to Mr. Thomas, which he pretended to have received from the Paishwa, containing orders enjoining him to assist Luckwa, who was declared to be the protector of the family of the deceased Scindiah, and directed to remain in the service of his widow. These letters Mr. Thomas knew to be forged, and was moreover well aware that Luckwa was at this time, as he had ever been, his declared and inveterate enemy; and on several occasions had endeavoured to overthrow his authority, by promising grants of his country in the Paishwa's name to other people. This behaviour induced Mr. Thomas to regret not having afforded aid to Simbonauth; as he might at this juncture not only have saved him, but crushed those who not long after effected his downfall.

Simbonauth had requested Mr. Thomas to come to his assistance, but without success.

Mr. Thomas however offered him an asylum within his own districts. He advised him not to think of resisting Mr. Perron with his present confused and disorderly force. This advice, though salutary, was of no avail; for

Simbonauth, confiding in the proteſtations of his followers, reſolved to remain in the Dooab, and wait the approach of the enemy. The event manifeſted the truth of Mr. Thomas's prediction; as on the actual appearance of the enemy, the troops of Simbonauth not only deſerted, but actually endeavoured by treacherous means to ſeize his perſon, and deliver him up a priſoner. Diſappointed in their treacherous deſigns, they went over to the enemy; but not before Simbonauth had fortunately effected his eſcape.

Repairing to the Punjab, he there ſought and obtained an aſylum in the diſtricts of Baug Sing, chief of Booreah.

At this time Mr. Thomas received intelligence that ſeveral of his diſtricts, particularly thoſe in the vicinity of Hanſi, were in a ſtate of actual rebellion, and had plundered the merchants reſorting to that place of a very conſiderable ſum of money, and other valuable effects. Among others concerned in this revolt, were the zemindars of Bulhalli, Sorani, Jumalpore, and Bhuwaul.

This last mentioned town is computed to contain ten thousand inhabitants, who retain a character so remarkable for bravery, that several armies have been defeated in attempting the reduction of that place. Among others, the late Ismaeel Beg, with sixteen thousand men, and one hundred pieces of cannon, besieged it for a long time in vain. The inhabitants are Rahtore Rajepoots, and possess the accustomed valour of that tribe; although this character has in some instances been sullied by a cruelty not usual among the rest of their brethren.

It being the rainy season when this rebellion broke out, and Mr. Thomas apprehending the most serious consequences if the cultivation of the lands was prevented, marched with all possible expedition towards the rebels, and first appeared before the town of Bulhalli.

In that place were three thousand men, who, although well armed, were badly supplied with provisions. He might, according to his usual custom, have stormed, but thinking from the number and bravery of the garrison the event might prove doubtful, had recourse to the surer means of reducing it by a blockade.

Having erected a chain of redoubts, well fortified and ſupplied with artillery, he completely encircled the place, encompaſſing the whole by a ditch twelve feet in depth. As no proviſions could enter the town, the garriſon after ſome days experienced diſtreſs; they made repeated ſallies, but having to croſs the ditch before they could reach the redoubts on the plain, they became expoſed to the whole fire of the trenches, and were in conſequence defeated in every ſucceſſive attack. To increaſe their annoyance, Mr. Thomas began to draw off the water from a neighbouring reſervoir, which reduced them to the neceſſity of drinking the water from the wells within the fort; this being bitter in its quality rendered it unwholeſome, and cauſed ſickneſs within the garriſon. Proviſions now became ſo ſcarce that nothing remained but damaged grain.

During the ſiege of this place the inhabitants of Bhowanee, a neighbouring town, had made ſeveral attempts to throw in ſuccours, but in vain. To retaliate upon them, Mr. Thomas ordered his cavalry to make excurſions in the neighbourhood of Bhowanee, and plunder the country. Their exertions were attended with ſucceſs: upwards of one hundred and fifty perſons were killed in reſiſting, and the cavalry brought away with them three thouſand head of cattle, which they depoſited ſafely in Mr. Thomas's camp. This laſt attack having deterred the people of Bhowanee from any further interruption, and no ſuccours as yet having arrived from Mr. Perron, the garriſon, ſeeing no likelihood of aſſiſtance from without, conſented to capitulate. Compoſed of people belonging to different villages, and having ſeparate intereſts to adjuſt, they could not come to any determination among themſelves. By this time, from the want of proviſions, from diſeaſe, and other cauſes, they were reduced to one third of their original number; even of the few that remained ſeveral were then ill. Mr. Thomas, deſirous of putting at end to theſe altercations, drew out his troops with intent to ſtorm the place; but the enemy perceiving his reſolution, at laſt conſented to capitulate; they agreed to pay him the ſum of 30,000 rupees, and to deliver up the fort with the property contained therein. Hoſtages having been taken for the performance of these articles, Mr. Thomas returned to Hansi, where he employed himself in completing ammunition and stores, fully determined to invade the Punjab, and punish the rajah of Pattialah, for his treacherous conduct in breaking the treaty, by affording aid to the Batties in the preceding year.

That chief (whose force consisted of fifteen hundred cavalry and one thousand infantry) was at this time besieging his sister in her fort. Assured of speedy relief, this gallant lady still continued to hold out; and Mr. Thomas's preparations being at length completed, he first marched to her relief. On his approach the rajah thought proper to raise the siege, and retire within the fortifications of Sonaum.* Thither he was followed by Mr. Thomas, who intended to have stormed the place; but the unexpected arrival of Tarah Sing, an ally, and son-in-law of the rajah, with a very consider-

* Sonaum, a large town, situated 22 coss to the westward of Pattialah.

able force, for the present prevented the attack.

By this time also the neighbouring peasantry having joined the rajah's standard, determined Mr. Thomas to relinquish his intention until a more favourable opportunity. Numerous bodies of cavalry continued daily to hover round the skirts of his army during the march, by which he sustained great annoyance. After a fatiguing march of four-and-twenty miles, on coming to the ground, he was surprised by the sound of the Thamuck.*

He encamped near the town of Bellud. A large body of the enemy, who were concealed in a neighbouring jungle, waited the event with impatience, and hoped to take advantage of the disorder of Mr. Thomas's troops, whilst attacked by the town's people, and cut them to pieces. It is here necessary to remark, that

* Thamuck, a large military drum, in common use in the north-west parts of India, the sounding of which is always considered as a prelude to hostilities.

in confequence of the continued ftate of warfare in thofe parts, the villages and towns are ftrongly fortified, and capable of making a defperate refiftance againft the attacks of their predatory neighbours.

The walls of the town aforementioned were nine feet thick, with a ditch twenty feet in depth, and the garrifon numerous. Mr. Thomas, therefore, without lofs of time, made preparations for ftorming before he could be attacked by the enemy. By a vigorous affault, he carried the place with the lofs of only eighty of his own people, though with upwards of five hundred of the enemy; and though he exerted every means in his power to prevent a continuance of the flaughter, he was unfuccefsful: the rancorous enmity which fubfifted between his own troops, who were moofulmauns, and the Seiks being fo great, that the former never omitted any opportunity of revenging themfelves on the latter in the fevereft manner.

The town's people who furvived the affault were ranfomed by a large fum of money. Mr.

Thomas's views were now directed to dividing the enemy's force, which consisted of ten thousand men, to raise contributions in the neighbouring districts, and also to explore the country. To effect these objects, he encamped in a centrical position between the towns of Pattialah and Sonaum. Desirous however of punishing Tarah Sing, whom, as we have before seen, had come to the assistance of the rajah, Mr. Thomas now determined to advance towards Malhere Kotela, the enemy's principal residence. This town is situate on the Punjab frontier; the road lay through a thick jungle, well adapted for an ambuscade. He was marching quietly along, when a smart firing was heard in the front of his line. Instantly repairing to the spot, he found that a party who had advanced to reconnoitre were attacked by a superior body of the enemy. By the time Mr. Thomas arrived, the party attacked had got out of the jungle to the entrance of an extensive plain; and he now perceived that the present assault had been made only with a view to call off his attention from he large and populous town of Bhaut.

This town was garrisoned by the troops of Tarah Sing, to the amount of three thousand men.

Mr. Thomas nevertheless resolved to storm it. The walls of the fort were twelve feet thick and thirty in height; four strong bastions, well fortified with cannon, commanding the town below, as well as the plain adjoining, it was in all respects a place difficult of access. Mr. Thomas himself, at the head of a select body of his troops, entered nearly opposite the centre of the town; whilst Mr. Hopkins, the son of a field officer in the East India Company's service, now in Mr. Thomas's employ, led on his party to storm the eastern angle. The affair was desperate; and though the town was soon set on fire, the enemy made a brave and determined resistance. Mr. Hopkins gallantly advancing to the attack, stormed in the quarter assigned him, though at the moment of success he was unfortunately shot through the body, and several other officers were killed or disabled, the enemy still keeping up a tremendous fire from the fort. The affair presented a doubtful aspect. A large body of cavalry making their appearance without the town, Mr. Thomas's troops, though in poſſeſſion of the place, whether from the exceſſive heat occaſioned by the ſurrounding flames, or the ſevere fire they ſuſtained from the enemy in the fort, were inclined to retreat. At that critical inſtant Mr. Thomas, having with the greateſt preſence of mind brought up a ſix-pounder cloſe to the gate of the fort, by repeated diſcharges almoſt demoliſhed it; the enemy then gave up the conteſt, and by ſubmiſſion ſaved a further effuſion of blood on both ſides.

The lives of the people within the fort were granted, but Mr. Thomas compelled them to pay him fifty thouſand rupees.

The chief of Malhere Kotelah now thought proper to change ſides; and being like other Patans, adopted the practice of his countrymen by connecting himſelf with the party from whom he expected to derive moſt advantage.

He agreed to pay Mr. Thomas a ſum of

money, and moreover ſent a body of troops under the command of his nephew to join him.

Kurrum Sing a Seik chief, and ruler of the diſtrict of Shahabad, had for ſome time been hoſtile towards Mr. Thomas; and though at his firſt ſettlement he had made profeſſions of friendſhip, very ſoon altered his conduct. To encourage his enmity towards Mr. Thomas, the rajah of Pattialah offered his daughter in marriage to the ſon of Kurrum Sing, and their union was followed by an open declaration of war. The troops of Pattialah were reinforced with five thouſand Seiks. On the junction of theſe troops, a grand council of war was held; and it was there reſolved that a general combination of the Seik chiefs ſhould be formed, to expel Mr. Thomas from the country. They conſidered him as a dangerous perſon, and well knew that if he was ſucceſsful on the preſent occaſion, they might hereafter expect the moſt ſerious ill conſequences to their tribe from his future incurſions.

Mr. Thomas, by his ſpies in the enemies'

camp, received correct information of all their deliberations, but had no apprehension for the event; being well convinced, that a body of men, though ever so numerous, being under the command of so many different leaders, each of them influenced by their own separate interest, were incapable of executing any plan with that degree of promptness which in military transactions can alone ensure success.

A circumstance now arose that turned the scale much in the enemy's favour.

Roy Kellaun, an independant chief on the north-western frontier of the Punjab,* and whose revenue amounted to five lacks of rupees, had lately died, and was succeeded by his eldest son Roy Elias, then a youth.

The Rannee, his mother, in consequence of the tender age of her son, thought proper to assume the reins of government; and though desirous of doing all the justice in her power, was, from inexperience, wholly unfit to transact

* Consult the map.

the affairs of her country. The neighbouring Seiks, who, during the life-time of the late rajah, had, through his policy and good management, continued on friendly terms, now perceiving the unprotected ſtate of his infant ſon, joined in invading his territories; which having plundered and overrun, they ſoon, with the exception of a few forts (from their natural ſtrength deemed inacceſſible) brought under ſubjection the greater part of the country. About this time Zemaun Shah, king of Cabul, arrived at Lahore, a city fifty coſs diſtant from the young rajah's capital. This proximity induced the princeſs regent to implore the aſſiſtance of that monarch, in reinſtating her ſon in his authority; and for that purpoſe ſhe accordingly diſpatched a vakeel to Lahore.

The Sieks, whether it roſe from a dread of being attacked by Zemaun Shah, or they were apprehenſive that aſſiſtance would be brought from another quarter, ſhortly after this event thought proper ſuddenly to evacuate the country, when the peaſantry returned to their allegiance. But now a new obſtacle aroſe, which not only prevented for the preſent a continuance of the Rannee's tranquillity, but plunged her into ſtill deeper misfortunes than thoſe ſhe had before experienced.

CHAPTER XIII.

Singular account of an impostor among the Seiks—His pretensions; he is detected by a Seik chief—Threatens Mr. Thomas—is compelled to fly—reduction of Kanhori—attack of Sefeedoo—termination of the campaign.

IN the Seik army was a man of the Cuttry tribe, ambitious, artful, and intriguing, and whose knowledge of mankind, from long and deep reflection, had convinced him it was no difficult matter to render his countrymen the dupes of his own artifices: this man, who pretended to trace his lineage from the great prophet Nanick, the founder and lawgiver of the Seiks, had a regular correspondence with some of his creatures in the Abdali camp, and from time to time received intelligence of the motions and intentions of Zemaun Shah. Informed by his emissaries that the Shah had determined to return to his own dominions, and the exact time being specified for his setting out, this artful impoſtor aſſembled the chiefs of the Seik army, and pretending to the gift of inſpiration, acquainted them that during the preceding night he had been favoured with a viſit from their prophet; who after lamenting the hardſhips under which his favourite tribe had laboured by the invaſion of Abdallis, he had, through the permiſſion of the Almighty, been enabled to prevail on Zemaun Shah to return to his own country, and that at the moment they were now diſcourſing that prince had actually commenced his march.

Surpriſed at the apparent abſurdity of this declaration, many of the chiefs treated the information with deſerved ridicule; but when at three o'clock in the afternoon of the ſame day, intelligence arrived of the actual march of the Shah, as predicted by the impoſtor, the whole army appeared ſtruck with contrition for their error, and inſiſted on their chiefs deprecating the anger of this deſcendant of Nanick, by expiatory offerings, and preſents of all kinds.

Fully ſatisfied with the ſucceſs of his ſtratagem, he now affected a lofty deportment, and it was with great difficulty that the chiefs prevailed on him to accept the proffered offerings; nor did he wholly relent until they offered to return with an army to Lodhana, and put him in possession of the country of the unfortunate Roy Elias; to this he not only yielded a ready assent, but added a falsehood to his former deceit, by informing the chiefs that the late invasion of the Shah had been solely owing to the intrigues of the Rannee, aided by the machinations of her neighbour the Patan chief of Malhere, who had invited the Abdalli Prince to take possession of the Punjab.

The Seik army daily increasing in numbers by accessions of the peasantry, who joined them from all quarters, now directed their march to Malhere, and resolved to begin their operations with the siege of that place.

The Patans who were in Malhere came out of the city to encounter the Seiks on the plain, but the presence of their pretended prophet inspiring them with more than usual confidence, the Patans were repulsed, and driven from the field with great ſlaughter; and the Seiks entering the town along with the fugitives, the place was quickly taken, while the few who remained, having quitted the city, ſought refuge in the fort of Kotelah.

The Seiks prepared to follow up their victory by laying ſiege to that place; and ſo great was the conſternation of the Patans, that though it was defended by a very high wall, a ditch, and contained a garriſon of 600 men, they were utterly unable to reſiſt; and had it not been for the aſſiſtance of their ally, the rajah of Pattialah, who ſent a body of his own troops for their protection, they muſt have ſurrendered at diſcretion.

This addition of force however rendered abortive all attempts of the Seiks to reduce Kotelah; they therefore ſeparated, though a conſiderable body, who to all appearance ſtill adhered to the impoſtor, diſperſed themſelves over the Rannee's country, of which, after much predatory warfare, they got poſſeſſion.

Reduced to a ſituation truly deplorable, that

princeſs had now recourſe to negotiation; and through the mediation of the chief of the Pattialah concluded a treaty with the Seiks, by which ſhe agreed to pay the ſum of two lacs of rupees, a part of which was depoſited in caſh, and the remainder in jewels, horſes, and warlike ſtores.

The impoſtor however, who ſtill had a large force, would agree to no terms but the actual ſurrender of the whole of the country; and though the young rajah, with a view to mollify the ſeverity of his demand, waited in perſon upon him, threw himſelf at his feet, and in terms moſt ſubmiſſive implored an abatement of his former reſolve, he continued inexorable.

In this ſtate of affairs the impoſtor, who had now got poſſeſſion of the perſon of the young rajah, refuſed to let him return to his mother, and declared he ſhould remain a priſoner until he complied with the terms propoſed.

But Kurrum Sing, one of the chiefs who had hitherto been in the ſervice of the impoſtor, now repented of his credulity, and resolved to protect the person of the rajah, and conduct him in safety to his own residence. This he resolutely effected, in spite of every effort to the contrary; he conducted the youth to Malhere, and there left him in quiet possession of his capital

This conduct excited much indignation in the impostor, who now took upon him to censure the behaviour of Kurrum Sing on all occasions, and to threaten him with the vengeance of heaven for thus opposing the views of an inspired person. Kurrum Sing however only waited for an opportunity to detect his hypocrisy, and expose him to the world, which fortunately soon happened.

To preserve the reputation he had thus acquired for sanctity, the impostor, among other tricks, used frequently, at night and by stealth, to deposit a vessel filled with sweetmeats under ground. This in the morning was produced to his followers as a present from the divinity, declaring at the same time that none ſhould partake of the contents but ſuch as vowed, to the utmoſt of their abilities, to join in the extermination of the Mooſſulman race, as enemies to their own prophet and his religion.

This farce was for a long time continued, and had ſerved to impreſs the minds of his followers with the higheſt reſpect and veneration for his character, but the time was now arrived for his detection. Kurrum Sing, who was well verſed in the arts and deceits practiſed by *fakeers* * upon the vulgar, directed ſome of his own people to repair privately to the place where the veſſel was depoſited; and after having thrown away the contents, to give a more effectual air of ridicule to the diſcovery, to replace them by a quantity of horſe dung. In the morning, when as uſual the veſſel was brought out, the company aſſembled ſhewed marks of the utmoſt horror and aſtoniſhment.

But the pretended prophet, not diſmayed by the accident, replied to their enquiries with a

* Itinerant mendicants.

ſedate and unruffled countenance, that the reaſon of this extraordinary change was manifeſt, as the great founder of their religion had choſen this method to evince his reſentment of their late impious conduct, in concluding a treaty with Mooſſulmaun chiefs, who were the acknowledged enemies of their own faith.

This harangue, however impudent, would have been attended with the deſired effect, had not Kurrum Sing at that inſtant ſtepped forth from the crowd of chiefs, by which the impoſtor was encircled, and in the moſt public manner, accompanied with ſarcaſtic obſervations and much levity, expoſed the whole of the deceit which he had cauſed to be practiſed the preceding night.

The charm was now diſſolved; the remaining chiefs, aſhamed of having ſubmitted to an impoſition ſo groſs, now abandoned him to his fate, and he was left with only about 1000 of his own people; but the peaſantry of the country, who from reſtleſſneſs of ſpirit are always ready to change their rulers, ſtill adhered to his intereſts, and having joined him in great numbers, brought with them an abundant ſupply of proviſions and other neceſſaries.

The Rannee, without protection, was in no condition to reſiſt; and the Seik chiefs, although they would no longer embrace the impoſtor's cauſe, were nevertheleſs unwilling to fight againſt him; he, therefore, ſoon got poſſeſſion of the Rannee's country, and had formed the ſiege of Lodhana,* about the ſame time that Mr. Thomas, as we have before related, made himſelf maſter of the fort of Bhaut.

It was in this ſituation of her affairs, when reduced almoſt to extremity, that the Rannee determined to apply to Mr. Thomas for his aſſiſtance in expelling the impoſtor from her territories. With this intention ſhe diſpatched a confidential ſervant to his camp, who, on her part, promiſed him a remuneration of a lack of rupees, if he would eſpouſe her cauſe, and re-

* Consult the map.

inſtate her ſon, the young rájah, in his authority.

She promiſed moreover to ſend him an annual tribute of 50,000 rupees, if he would guarantee her ſon in the undiſturbed poſſeſſion of it.

Mr. Thomas, though well aware that by accepting the preſent offer he ſhould draw on himſelf a procraſtinated war, nevertheleſs obſerves with that humane conſideration which always marked his character, that the fallen condition of an ancient and honourable family had great weight with him in forming his reſolution on this head.

In the mean time the impoſtor, hearing of the negotiations betwixt the Rannee and Mr. Thomas, ſent the latter a letter, in which he ſtated, that having called to his aſſiſtance Runjeet Sing and others, the moſt powerful among the Seik chiefs, he was now on his march againſt Mr. Thomas, and adviſed him, if he wiſhed for quarter, to ſend a vakeel directly to his camp. In this letter, arrogating to himſelf the title of ſucceſſor of Nanick, and ſovereign of the Seik nation, he recommended implicit obedience to his commands. Equally indignant at the ſtyle of the impoſtor's addreſs, as he was regardleſs of his menaces, Mr. Thomas replied, that had he feared the power of the Seiks he would not have penetrated thus far into the Punjab; that he was accuſtomed to receive and not to ſend vakeels; and that if the impoſtor wiſhed to live on amicable terms, he muſt not only pay a ſum of money, as others had been compelled to do, but likewiſe immediately evacuate the territories which he had ſo unjuſtly uſurped from the infant rajah.

The boldneſs of this anſwer only contributed to incenſe the impoſtor, and he prepared to attack Mr. Thomas.

Meanwhile the young rajah, deſpairing of profiting by a longer ſtay with the chief of Pattialah, of his own accord took leave, and came ſtraight to Mr. Thomas's camp. "The "comely appearance (ſays he) of this youth, "his fallen condition, and, above all, the con-

" fidence he ſhewed in placing his whole re-
" liance on one againſt whom he was ſo lately
" leagued in enmity, altogether influenced me
" in his ſavour, and determined me to uſe
" every exertion in ſupport of his cauſe."

The impoſtor, who by this time had reinforced his army with the troops of Pattialah and others, was encamped in the neighbourhood; but, on Mr. Thomas's advancing, he thought proper to retreat; and his people having no artillery, evacuated the different poſts much faſter than Mr. Thomas could advance to take poſſeſſion. So rapid was his march, that in one place he found the bed, palankeen, tent, and baggage, belonging to the impoſtor, who by a timely retreat ſaved himſelf from being made priſoner, and never afterwards occaſioned any diſturbance.

The Rannee and her ſon were put in poſſeſſion of their country, the moſt active of the rebels were ſeized, and it was not long before the rajah's authority was completely re-eſtabliſhed.

During theſe tranſactions, the chief of Pattialah, having been joined by others, advanced to attack Mr. Thomas, with a determination to expel him the country. Several ſkirmiſhes enſued between the armies, but without much effect on either ſide, neither party being deſirous of riſking a general engagement. The war was therefore carried on in a deſultory manner. The Seiks wiſhed, by annoying his foraging parties, to cut off the ſupplies from his camp. This mode alſo prevented him from making collections; and though nothing ſerious occurred, yet the ſcene of action being on the borders of the young rajah's country, occaſioned great loſs to the cultivation of the lands. Mr. Thomas, therefore, would willingly have carried the war immediately into the enemy's territories. To this, however, neither the rajah or his mother would conſent; but, with the moſt preſſing intreaties, requeſted him to remain, while the Seiks continued in that neighbourhood.

So long as prudence allowed, Mr. Thomas willingly liſtened to the ſolicitations of his allies; but his ammunition beginning to fall ſhort, he was reluctantly compelled to march toward his own country to procure a ſupply.

The Seiks, as he had foreſeen, haraſſed him on the march; but their attempts proving ineffectual to do him any eſſential injury, only incited him to retaliate, by deſtroying their villages as he paſſed along. Directing his march towards Hanſi, he perceived, not without ſatisfaction, that the whole of the Seik army were following him, by which means the country of his youthful ally would, at leaſt for the preſent, be free from their depredations.

It muſt now be remarked, that previous to Mr. Thomas's ſetting out for the Punjab frontier, the chiefs of Keithul and Jeind, two of his moſt powerful neighbours, had concluded a treaty, by which they agreed to a ceſſation of hoſtilities during his abſence, to abſtain from the invaſion of his territories, and allow him to proſecute the war againſt his enemies. Thoſe chiefs, perceiving the ſtrong combination which had been formed againſt Mr. Thomas, now joined themſelves to his other enemies. He therefore prepared to puniſh them.

Having, by forced marches, got ahead of the Seik army, Mr. Thomas firſt led his troops againſt the fort of Kanhori, which he took by ſtorm, and put the garriſon to the ſword.

The acquiſition of this fortreſs, which was only thirty coſs diſtant from Pattialah, was of great conſequence to him. Situated on the borders of his own territory, and near the Cuggur river, it appeared ſo well calculated for a depoſit of ſtores and ammunition, that he repaired the fortifications, and placed in it a ſtrong garriſon. Then collecting hoſtages from the neighbouring diſtricts, as ſecurity for their future pacific intentions, he marched to Retara, another ſtrong place on the frontier, belonging to Lall Sing. The garriſon conſiſted of five hundred men; but before a breach could be effected, dreading the fate of the inhabitants of Kanhori, they aſked for quarter, and were allowed by Mr. Thomas to march out with the honours of war.

From this place he proſecuted his route towards Hanſi. The hot ſeaſon being now far advanced, the Seiks, through want of water and forage for their cattle, were compelled to relinquish the pursuit; and, drawing off their force, encamped in the neighbourhood of Keithul, there to wait until the approaching rains permitted a renewal of hostilities.

Mr. Thomas next marched into the district of Jeind, from whence he exacted tribute, and took hostages; but, from a dearth of water in this neighbourhood to supply his troops, he did not think proper at that time to attack it.

During his absence in the Punjab, Bappoo Scindiah, agreeably to instructions received from Mr. Perron, invaded Mr. Thomas's possessions; but hearing of his return, thought proper to fall back upon the main army, at this time encamped near Delhi.

Mr. Thomas next marched, and laid siege to Sefeedoo, a town dependant upon the chief of Jeind. This place was built of brick, and the walls of uncommon height. Having erected three redoubts, in which he placed eighteen cannon, twelve and ſix pounders, he began to batter the fort, and kept up an inceſſant fire until three o'clock in the afternoon. At this time, fearing that the place might be reinforced during the enſuing night, Mr. Thomas determined on an immediate aſſault. The garriſon conſiſted of ſeven hundred men, three hundred of which remained within the fort; and the reſt ſallying out, deſcended into the ditch, which croſſing with rapidity, they commenced an attack upon Mr. Thomas's advanced poſts; but moſt of the party, among whom were ſome chiefs of diſtinction, were put to the ſword. Mr. Thomas's ſoldiers in their turn attempted to mount the breach; but the ſcaling ladders being found too ſhort, and the ſtorming party at the ſame inſtant aſſailed by the remainder of the troops within the garriſon, theſe gallant men were involved in the greateſt difficulty, and entirely expoſed to the enemy's ſhot, which fell ſo thick among them, and did ſo much execution, that, after a deſperate and hard fought conflict of two hours, Mr. Thomas was compelled to retire, with the loſs of four hundred and fifty of his beſt men.

The gallant Mr. Hopkins, who had been conſpicuous for his ardour throughout the attack, on this occaſion received another ſevere wound.

The enemy, who had likewiſe ſuffered greatly, now attempted to eſcape from the fort, and to cut their way through Mr. Thomas's troops. This, notwithſtanding every exertion on his part, they effected; and having taken ſhelter in a thick foreſt in the neighbourhood, Mr. Thomas thought it uſeleſs to purſue them any longer, but returned to take poſſeſſion of the fort.

During this tranſaction, the Seik army lay within eighteen coſs, and that of Bappoo Scindiah only nine, though both, happily for Mr. Thomas, remained quiet.

He next marched to Kythul. Here the rajah of Pattialah and others of the Seik chiefs, ſent vakeels into his camp to negotiate a peace. Mr. Thomas, on his part, was ſincerely inclined to put an end to the war, as he was well informed that the army of Mr. Perron was now on its march from Delhi, for the avowed purpose of affording aid to the Seiks. They likewise had recently been informed that disturbances prevailed in their own country, and therefore hastened to conclude the present negotiations. It was agreed, therefore, that the Seiks should pay the sum of 1,35,000 rupees, and renounce all pretensions to the country of Roy Kellaun; that the rajah of Pattialah should be reconciled to his sister, with whom he had been so long at variance; that this lady should be reimbursed for the property that had been confiscated; that certain districts should be ceded to Mr. Thomas; and finally, that the rajah of Pattialah should keep two battalions of infantry in constant pay, who were to be stationed for the defence of the Punjaub frontier, as a mutual safeguard to either party.

" Thus (says Mr. Thomas, in his usual manly and energetic strain,) ended a campaign of seven months, in which I had been more successful than I could possibly have expected

" when I firſt took the field with a force " conſiſting of five thouſand men, and thirty-" ſix pieces of cannon. I loſt in killed, wound-" ed, and diſabled, nearly one third of my " force; but the enemy loſt five thouſand per-" ſons of all deſcriptions. I realiſed near two " hundred thouſand rupees, excluſive of the " pay of my army, and was to receive an ad-" ditional one hundred thouſand for the hoſ-" tages which were delivered up. I explored " the country, formed alliances, and, in ſhort, " was dictator in all the countries belonging to " the Seiks, ſouth of the river Sutledge.*

* Before we take leave of this interesting country, it may not be improper to advert to two of the desiderata of Major Rennel, which, from a perusal of his excellent Memoir accompanying the map of Hindoostan, appear to be as follow:

First, to ascertain the existence of a canal, which was to have been cut by the order of the emperor Firose, from the river Sutledge to the Jumna, the execution of which design would have opened a communication by water from Cabul to Assam.

Second, the altars of Alexander, which, according to Arrian, must have been situated between the Beyah and the Sutledge, near the modern city of Ferozepore.

It is much to be regretted that the spirit of modern travel has not yet reached these distant, though, to the British nation, not wholly inaccessible regions, as no doubt many very curious particulars in ancient history, which have hitherto remained in obscurity, might, by diligent and accurate investigation, be brought to light.

CHAPTER XIV.

Reflections—Combination formed against Mr. Thomas—commencement of hostilities—battle with Captain Smith—death of Mr. Hopkins—Mr. Thomas's opponents become more and more formidable—treacherous designs of his officers—multiplied difficulties—Mr. Thomas is compelled to fly—reaches Hansi—he capitulates—arrives at the British frontier—his death and character.

LIKE a sea-worn mariner, who, after encountering the dangers and hardships of a long and tedious voyage, is at length gratified with the sight of land; or as a benighted traveller on his road after a weary journey, losing himself in desert wilds, or betrayed by false tracts in the treacherous snow, looks forward to the enjoyments of his peaceful home; so are we happy to perceive a prospect of terminating our labours, in view of a desired haven.

To this haven, after a little more toſſing on the tempeſtuous ocean of life, and a few more viciſſitudes of fortune, we are anxious to conduct our friend and hero; and, after ſharing with him the perils and dangers of the voyage, finally to place him in that Aſylum, where every trouble is forgotten, and where every ſorrow ceaſes to exiſt.

However flattering might appear the termination of the campaign, Mr. Thomas's good fortune may, at this period, be ſaid to have attained its meridian ſplendour; ſince a dark cloud, which had long been gathering over his head, was now preparing to discharge its malignant contents: its baneful influence threatened even the utter extirpation of thoſe hopes of fortune and independance by which he had ſo long been buoyed up, and which had therefore taken deep root in his aſpiring mind.

But as the combination which was about to be formed againſt him was in the end productive of his downfall, and the death blow to his hopes, it will be neceſſary in this place to take a retroſpective ſurvey of the ſtrength and resources of that part of the Mahratta empire, with which he was entering on an interesting and eventful warfare.

This will equally enable us to comprehend the situation of his numerous and powerful enemies, as to appreciate the exertion of those faculties and talents which were now called forth, and which place his last struggles for the support of his authority in a point of view highly creditable to his general character. On the death of Madhajee Scindiah in 1794, he was succeeded in his possessions and authority by his nephew Dowlut Row Scindiah. This youth, though of promising parts, was by no means equal in capacity to his renowned uncle.

That politic prince, aware of the advantages to be derived from the practice of the European system of tactics, and the introduction of military discipline into his armies, had, by the assistance of General Duboign, raised several brigades of infantry, which he left entire to his nephew. Shortly after his elevation, Dowlut Row constituted Mr. Perron his commander-in-chief, whoſe influence has continued to ſway the mind of his maſter from that period until the preſent time.

The force thus raiſed amounted to forty thouſand infantry, thirty thouſand cavalry, with five hundred pieces of heavy artillery.

This acceſſion of force, though diſperſed over an extenſive tract of country, the fruits of the late Scindiah's conqueſts, could, when circumſtances required, be brought to act in concert.

On the other ſide, Holkar, the ruler of Indore, (a province ſituated in the centre of the Dekan) could at this time command an army of fifty thouſand men, with three hundred pieces of cannon; and laſtly, the Seiks, who, as we have already ſeen, were able to bring into the field nearly an equal number.

Holkar, however, not being at variance with Mr. Thomas, muſt not therefore be numbered among his enemies, though the prodigious acceſſion of force againſt him, in an union of the

Seiks and Scindiah, was of itſelf ſufficient to aſtound and overwhelm him.

To counteract the deſigns of his enemies, Mr. Thomas, at the period we are ſpeaking of, had an army whoſe utmoſt force conſiſted of eight battalions of infantry, amounting in all to ſix thouſand men, fifty pieces of cannon, well appointed and well ſerved, one thouſand cavalry, and fifteen hundred Rohillahs, with about two thouſand men, who garriſoned his different forts; but with this force, comparatively ſo ſmall, he had a ſpirit and elevation of mind not to be ſubdued by accident, or depreſſed by ill fortune; and not only waited the event with firmneſs, but declared previous to the commencement of hoſtilities, that if his reſources in money did not fail, he doubted not with his preſent army to hold out againſt the efforts of all the native princes of India.

To preſerve, however, the thread of our narration, it will now be neceſſary to remark, that repeated letters had lately been ſent by Scindiah to Mr. Thomas, to induce him to act in conjunction with Mr. Perron against their common enemies.

In anſwer, he repreſented that Mr. Perron and himſelf being ſubjects of different nations, then in a ſtate of actual hoſtility againſt each other, it was impoſſible they could ever act in concert, or with cordiality. He was moreover convinced, that as a Frenchman, and poſſeſſed of a national enmity againſt him, Mr. Perron would always be induced to repreſent his actions in a light moſt unfavourable to his intereſts: that principles of honour, on the preſent occaſion, forbad his acting under the command of a Frenchman: but if Scindiah was really deſirous of employing him to the advantage of the ſtate, or to his own benefit, he might beſtow on him a ſeparate command, under the control of a Mahratta general; or, concludes Mr. Thomas with much ſpirit, "ſhould you "think proper to appoint me to the ma- "nagement of operations, either offenſive or "defenſive, in any part of the Dekan, Hin- "dooſtan, or Punjaub, I am ready and willing "to undertake the charge, ſo ſoon as the ne-

" ceſſary arrangements for the payment of " my troops can be completed."

In reply to this repreſentation, Scindiah, who had been tutored for the occaſion by Mr. Perron, urged in the ſtrongeſt manner the impoſſibility of conſenting to Mr. Thomas's requeſt, as it would ſerve as an unfavourable precedent; he recommended moreover, that in the preſent inſtance the national enmity of theſe commanders ſhould be laid aſide; and their mutual exertions made for the general benefit of the ſervice, but at all events deſired Mr. Thomas to ſuſpend his reſolution until his own arrival in Hindooſtan.

Some time after the above correſpondence, Mr. Perron wrote to Mr. Thomas, requeſting him to ſend a vakeel to confer upon the ſubject, for the mutual benefit of either party.

This requeſt was inſtantly complied with; and Mr. Thomas's vakeel, having received the neceſſary inſtructions, was diſpatched to Delhi. Arriving at Mr. Perron's camp, which was pitched in the neighbourhood of that city, he was received in a manner the moſt cordial and flattering.

The affairs of Scindiah were at this time in a ſituation that by no means juſtified a protracted war in his poſſeſſions in Hindooſtan, being himſelf engaged in an eventful and difficult conteſt with his ancient enemy Jeſſwunt Row Holkar.

The cautious chief therefore thought that to temporiſe with Mr. Thomas would be the moſt eligible method; as he might, in the courſe of his preſent warfare, have occaſion for the ſervices of Mr. Perron's troops.

In his maſter's name, therefore, Mr. Perron requeſted an interview. The fort of Behadur Ghur was the place named for the meeting. On his approach to that place, Mr. Thomas was informed that Perron had put to death a Seik chief, who had lately revolted from Scindiah, and of whoſe perſon he had got poſſeſſion by treacherous means.

This intelligence induced Mr. Thomas to obſerve the greateſt circumſpection in the approaching interview. Captain Smith, the ſon of an officer in the honourable Eaſt India Company's ſerviee, was diſpatched by Mr. Perron to meet and conduct him to the Mahratta camp. Mr. Thomas took along with him on this occaſion 300 cavalry, and two of his moſt approved battalions; being determined to afford no opportunity to his enemies to effect his ruin by treacherous means.

In the month of September, after ſome previous negociation between the parties, Mr. Perron and Mr. Thomas met for the firſt time at the town of Behadur Ghur. Mr. Thomas having received recent information that the affairs of Scindiah preſented an unfavourable aſpect, and that that chief was unequal to the conteſt with Jeſſwunt Row Holkar, hoped the preſent interview would be productive of an amicable adjuſtment of all former differences, and eſtabliſh the future tranquillity and good underſtanding of both parties.

In this, however, he was deceived; for at the

second day's meeting he was much surprised by a demand, equally sudden as unsuspected, from Mr. Perron, requesting him to give up the district of Jyjur entirely to the Mahrattas; in lieu of this he was to receive for the support of his battalions the monthly sum of 50,000 rupees, and henceforth to be considered as the immediate servant of Dowlut Row Scindiah.

Although this proposal might have been foreseen, Mr. Thomas gave it a positive denial; and perceiving the nature of the design formed against him, was aware that he should be required to act against Holkar in the present war; and if it proved unfavourable to the interests of that chief, and his authority was subverted, Scindiah would not only discontinue the payment of the monthly sum now offered to Mr. Thomas, but compel him to accept of any terms the Mahratta Government might think proper to impose.

For these reasons Mr. Thomas, without further discussion on the subject, abruptly broke up the conference, and marched away in disgust.

Pacific meaſures being now at an end, Mr. Perron, to begin the war with advantage, repaired directly to Jyjur, of which, being unfortified, he immediately took poſſeſſion. Mr. Thomas had ſtill left the fort of George Ghur, in which having ſtationed 800 men, he expected it would hold out a conſiderable time, nor was he deceived. La Fontaine, a commander in Mr. Perron's ſervice, having approached that place in the hope of taking it by aſſault, was ſo warmly received by the garriſon as to be compelled to retreat with conſiderable loſs.

The period, however, of Mr. Thomas's final diſcomfiture was not far off. His enemies preſſed on him on all ſides with accumulated vigour; and private treachery coming in aid of public misfortune, he was ſoon reduced to a ſituation the moſt painfully diſtreſſing.

The force of Mr. Perron at this time conſiſted of ten battalions of infantry, ſix thouſand horſe, a body of Rohillas, and ſixty pieces of heavy artillery. The Seiks were likewiſe preparing to ſend againſt him a conſiderable force; and in addition to theſe threatened evils, ſeveral of his own diſtricts perceiving the diſaſtrous ſituation of his affairs, joined their efforts to thoſe of his enemies.

A part of Mr. Perron's forces was commanded by Captain Smith, whom we have before had occaſion to notice, while a second diviſion was led by Mr. Lewis.

On his arrival at Hanſi, Mr. Thomas loſt no time in completing his ammunition and other ſtores; his intention was firſt to attack Mr. Lewis, but Captain Smith having lately inveſted the fort of George Ghur, by which means the collections in that diſtrict were interrupted, he reſolved to proceed to its relief.

George Ghur* is a ſmall fort erected by Mr. Thomas, when he firſt took poſſeſſion of the pergunnahs made over to him by Appakandarow; it is ſituated four coſs ſouth of Jyjur, and thirty diſtant from Delhi. The unquiet ſtate of the pergunnahs had induced Mr.

* For this account of the position of George Ghur, I am indebted to the kindness of my friend Captain Salkeld of the cavalry.

Thomas to erect this fort with a view to overawe the neighbouring villages, and when finished he placed a strong body of troops in it for its defence.

Mr. Thomas having left a body of Rohillas to defend Hansi, advanced towards Captain Smith, and after a march of eleven coss, encamped at the town of Mahim; Mr. Lewis at this time being seventeen coss to the northwest of that place.

Here he was informed that Captain Smith, who had got imperfect intelligence of his advance, had withdrawn his guns from the batteries and struck his camp.

Mr. Thomas having ordered the cavalry to proceed with all expedition, continued his march with the infantry towards George Ghur, where, on his arrival late in the evening, he learnt that Captain Smith had retreated.

Early on the ensuing morning Mr. Thomas commenced the pursuit, but Murtuza Khawn, the commandant of his second regiment, who had received orders to proceed in advance, and cut off the retreat of Captain Smith, most unaccountably lost his road, and the soldiers being fatigued, did not come up with their colours; with the only battalion that remained Mr. Thomas, on reaching the rear of Captain Smith's line of march, commenced the attack. Captain, Smith in order to cover the retreat of his artillery and baggage, drew up to receive Mr. Thomas, and after a slight cannonade continued his route; at this time Mr. Thomas's second regiment made its appearance, of which, from the causes before stated, not more than seventy men had yet come up, and they advancing incautiously into a field of joar* on the right, without having previously reconnoitred, were suddenly attacked by a battalion of the enemy; his men being so few in number made but a feeble resistance, and before they had time to unlimber, the enemy took possession of four of their guns.

Mr. Thomas hearing of this disaster, immediately advanced to the relief of his troops; he

* A grain very common in India.

was attended on this occasion by Asalut Khawn, a native officer, formerly in the service of the East India Company; they charged the enemy with vigour sword in hand, and after a severe conflict, in which the commandant of the enemy was taken prisoner, gave them a complete defeat.

Mr. Thomas's men, thinned in their numbers, and exhausted with fatigue, were unable to continue the pursuit; he sent his cavalry however after the fugitives, who picked up several stands of colours and small arms, which had been thrown away in the retreat.

In this encounter the enemy lost seven hundred men, while that of Mr. Thomas did not exceed one hundred; and had it not been for the soldier-like precautions taken by Captain Smith in sending forward his artillery and baggage, while he made head against Mr. Thomas with his infantry, the whole would inevitably have been captured; as it was, he lost the greater part of his ammunition and baggage.

Captain Smith on his defeat returned to Jyjur, and Mr. Thomas pitched his camp about two miles diſtant from that place.

In the morning he was preparing for a ſecond attack, when his hircarrahs, who had been on the look-out, brought intelligence of the approach of Mr. Lewis from an oppoſite direction, and his own troops being not only fatigued, but many of them diſperſed in ſearch of plunder, he did not think it adviſable at that time to hazard an engagement.

Mr. Thomas now returned to George Ghur, but had ſcarcely reached that place when he received intelligence of Mr. Perron's army having arrived at Byree, three coſs from his own encampment.

On the enſuing morning the enemy prepared to attack him. His ſituation was at this time critical; the battalions who had before retreated from George Ghur now came back, and took poſt within cannon ſhot to the eaſtward of his encampment; the force under Mr. Lewis was ſtationed to the ſouth-weſt;

while the enemy's numerous cavalry attacked him in front.

About four o'clock in the afternoon the action commenced by a heavy cannonade on both ſides; the motions of the enemy had induced Mr. Thomas to divide his army according to the ground he occupied, the advantage of which, allowing for the quality of the troops, was much in his favor; but his battalions not being accuſtomed to be expoſed to a cannonade, he drew up his army on a looſe ſand, which thereby deadened the ſhot and prevented their riſing after the firſt graze.

His force conſiſted of ten battalions of infantry, fifty pieces of cannon, ſix hundred Rohillas, and about five hundred cavalry, not exceeding in the aggregate five thouſand men; of which number only four thouſand could be brought into action.

Of this force five battalions were oppoſed to Mr. Lewis, two were aſſigned for the battalions oppoſite the centre of his line, and three to ſuſtain the ſhock of the enemy's horſe. On the commencement of the action Mr. Lewis's division came on briskly, having their guns at the drag ropes; Mr. Thomas, by a rapid discharge of round and grape shot from his artillery, at first threw them into confusion, and had he been able at this moment to prevent his troops from giving way, would have entirely defeated the enemy; but the centre of his line at this time being hard pressed by the enemy's cavalry, gave way, and no effort could prevent the remainder from following their example.

This rendered an immediate and spirited advance necessary to support. For this purpose Mr. Thomas ordered Mr. Hopkins, with the right wing, and Mr. Birch with the left, to advance and charge with bayonets in their respective wings; which service they performed with no less gallantry than success.

The enemy halted, and began to retreat; but a heavy fire being still continued from their numerous and well-served artillery, Mr. Thomas's people fell in great numbers, which the enemy's cavalry perceiving charged a second time.

They were not only repulſed with loſs, but purſued by Mr. Thomas's horſe to a conſiderable diſtance from the field of battle. At this time intelligence was brought to Mr. Thomas, who was on the left wing, that Mr. Hopkins had received a ſevere contuſion by a cannon ſhot, which broke his leg. This circumſtance ſo diſheartened his men, that they fell back in diſorder, and increaſed the confuſion in the centre of his line.

A ſtrong detachment of the enemy, who were ſtationed in Mr. Thomas's rear, prevented his receiving any ſupport from the troops oppoſed to them, and he could only ſpare one battalion to ſupport the centre. This body, however, conducted themſelves with ſo much gallantry, that could Mr. Thomas have afforded the additional aid of one hundred reſolute men, they might have advanced, and would in all probability have decided the fate of the day.

Night approaching, and his people being fatigued with the ſevere ſervice they had undergone, deſerted their colours, and took ſhelter in the neighbouring ravines.

Mr. Thomas exerted every effort to rally them, but without effect. In this exigency he called in a body of Rohillas, who had been stationed in an adjoining village, for the protection of the baggage; and to stimulate their exertions to a renewal of the attack, proffered, but in vain, a large increase of pay.

Both armies now drew off, and during the night lay on their arms; and the next morning, after a short and but distant cannonade, the enemy left Mr. Thomas master of the field of battle.

In this action, the enemy lost two thousand men, and thirty pieces of artillery. Mr. Thomas's loss was seven hundred men, and twenty pieces of cannon rendered unfit for further service. The cause of this loss in artillery was occasioned partly by his cannon being dismounted by the enemy's shot, and partly by the breaking of their axle-trees, as the carriages of the guns, instead of recoiling as usual after the discharge, from the nature of the soil, being a deep and heavy sand, stopt short and broke.

A few days after this action, the gallant Mr. Hopkins died of his wounds. The death of this young man was a great loss to Mr. Thomas's interests; and the firmness of his behaviour during the whole of his service, as well as the manly resignation which he exhibited at the close of life, stamps his character as an amiable man, a brave and gallant soldier.*

The enemy were daily reinforced by considerable numbers; among the first of whom were the troops under Bappoo Scindiah. Goordut Sing, Bunga Sing, Jonde Sing, and several other Seik chieftains, added their forces on the present occasion, Runjeet Sing, also ruler of Burtpoor, the Hattrass Rajah, Ramdeen of

* To do justice to the memory of my friend, I cannot, on this occasion, forbear to mention, that after the death of the gallant youth, Mr. Thomas, with a liberality of spirit which reflects the highest credit on his character, sent the young man's disconsolate sister (then become an orphan by her father's death) a present of two thousand rupees; with a promise if that sum was not thought sufficient to supply her wants, to extend his benevolence, though out of the remains of a ruined fortune of his own.

Kàtheler, and the troops of Rajah Ramdial, and Neen Sing, from the northern parts of the Dooab, completed this formidable aggregate.

Thirty thousand men, and a train of one hundred and ten pieces of artillery, had now surrounded Mr. Thomas on all sides: they so much overawed the neighbouring peasantry, that they not only immediately submitted, but discontinued their usual supplies of provisions for his camp, by which means his difficulties were so severely augmented, that all he could hope for, was an immediate attack on his camp, thereby to afford him an opportunity of evincing the bravery of his small force, by a vigorous and decisive encounter.

But being too weak to draw out his force in the open field, he was compelled to remain within his lines, and fortify the camp in the best possible manner, by drawing round it a hedge of the same kind of thorn-trees he had made use of when under similar embarrassment in the Jypoor dominions.

Having provided for the security of his camp,

and poſſeſſing a ſtock of proviſions ſufficient for a month's conſumption, he determined to remain in his preſent poſition until aſſiſtance could arrive from Luckwah, who, on the commencement of hoſtilities, had given him aſſurances of coming to his ſupport.

On the right of his encampment, a diviſion of Mr. Perron's force had thrown up ſome entrenched works; but Mr. Thomas, by a briſk fire from his guns, quickly compelled them to abandon it, which, favoured by the darkneſs of the night, they accompliſhed.

Skirmiſhes between the armies daily took place, in which the troops of Mr. Thomas, though much inferior in point of numbers, had manifeſtly the advantage.

The enemy's cavalry conſtantly hovered round his camp to annoy his foraging parties, and prevent ſupplies of proviſions from getting in. Though inferior to the enemy in point of numbers, Mr. Thomas's cavalry, from active and conſtant ſervice, had a decided advantage; and ſo very alert were his people, that two of the principal commanders of the enemy narrowly escaped being made prisoners in an attempt to surprise his camp.

Warned at length by experience that nothing was to be gained by these desultory attacks, and that Mr. Thomas strenuously persevered in his system of keeping close within his lines, they endeavoured to effect by corrupt and treacherous means, what they had vainly hoped to accomplish by open and manly warfare.

It must here be remarked, that the families of several of Mr. Thomas's officers resided within Mr. Perron's districts. He, in order to avail himself of their dependant situation, and accelerate Mr. Thomas's ruin, had, at the commencement of hostilities, placed a guard over their respective houses. Among the principal were the families of Shah Tab Khawn and Khirrate Khawn, the former a collector of Mr. Thomas's revenue, and the latter the commandant of his first matchlock regiment.

These men, who had been at first confined

by Mr. Perron, were afterwards liberated and ſent for by him to the fort of Coel, his place of reſidence.

He there, by preſent bribes and ſtill larger promiſes of reward in future, perſuaded them to join in effecting the ruin of their principal. The ungrateful men, although they had on various occaſions experienced the greateſt proofs of kindneſs and benevolence from Mr. Thomas, and whom he had raiſed from low ſituations in his army to authority and command, ſcrupled not to deſert him in the hour of his diſtreſs, and to join with his enemies in haſtening his downfal.

Their opportunities to effect this were too favourable. Shah Tab Khan, who commanded in the fort of George Ghur, had cauſed ſome ſtacks of hay within the fort, which formed the chief ſupport of his cattle, to be treacherouſly ſet on fire. The ſmall ſupply of grain alſo, which now conſtituted the ſupport of the garriſon, was privately made away with by means equally nefarious.

Not content with the effect already produced on the minds of Mr. Thomas's people by circumstances so untoward, these perfidious men were constantly instilling into the minds of the troops the perilousness of their situation, and apparent impossibility of ever extricating themselves, except by submission to the enemy and uniting with them. Of these treacherous designs Mr. Thomas was not informed until it was too late to frustrate their effect by any exertions on his part. Luckwah, whom he impatiently expected, did not arrive; and other chiefs who had promised their assistance, not only withheld it, but actually joined his enemies. About this time, likewise, Colonel Hessing, the commandant of Agra, arrived, and added himself to the number of Mr. Thomas's foes.

Several of his officers, whose habitations were in Mr. Perron's districts, deserted from his camp. His cattle were either killed or disabled, his grain had failed, and his ammunition fell short. With the utmost exertion he was scarcely able to procure grain by detaching parties secretly at night, who brought him in a ſcanty ſupply in the morning, though not without frequent diminution of his ſmall force in cavalry.

In this diſtreſs Mr. Thomas had no reſource but either to attack the enemy by night, to ſally forth and try the event of a conteſt in the day, or, attended by his cavalry, to attempt his retreat, leaving the infantry to make the beſt terms they could with the enemy.

After mature deliberation, he reſolved to attack the enemy, and force his way to Hanſi, which if he could reach in ſafety, he hoped to be able to continue his reſiſtance with effect, until aſſiſtance ſhould arrive from Luckwah.

He accordingly gave the neceſſary directions for carrying this reſolution into effect: but his people, ſuſpecting his intention of returning to Hanſi, now began to pack up their baggage and openly to deſert the camp.

On receiving intimation of this deſign, Mr. Thomas aſſembled the officers, and enquired of them the cauſe of this commotion. He was informed that no reliance could be placed on the ſoldiers, who, disheartened at their ſituation and the diſtreſs they daily endured, would no longer remain with their colours.

To quiet their apprehenſions, and reſtore confidence with regard to his ſuppoſed march to Hanſi, Mr. Thomas himſelf remained within the lines; and to encourage the drooping ſpirit of his people gave orders for an attack to be made on one of the enemy's advanced poſts, which from its ſituation appeared eaſy to be taken.

At this moment a difficulty aroſe regarding the bullock-drivers, who had deſerted the camp. Some ſepoys however, encouraged by the promiſe of liberal reward, undertook the office, and a ſelect detachment quitted the camp.

But whether from being infected with the general depreſſion of ſpirits that prevailed throughout the troops, or that they were really unfit for the occupation, the ſepoys conducted themſelves in ſo aukward a manner, and made ſo little exertion in getting on the guns, that

Mr. Thomas thought it more prudent to récal the detachment altogether, and it accordingly returned to camp.

Shortly after his hircarrahs brought information that the enemy, having been apprifed of his intention to force his way to Hanfi, had got their line under arms ready to oppofe his progrefs; and which, if he had attempted it in the prefent difcontented ftate of his troops, would in all probability have terminated in his difgrace.

Deftitute of forage, in want of ammunition, there being no poffibility of any fupply arriving from without, his foldiers daily deferting, and the few who remained even refufing to fight, except in the actual defence of the camp, in this fituation Mr. Thomas affembled a council of his officers, who, on his fubmitting to them the circumftances, gave it as their unanimous opinion, that there was nothing to be done but by an unconditional furrender to the enemy.

Mr. Thomas endeavoured to perfuade them that a retreat to Hanfi was ftill practicable;

but his exertions were ineffectual, and a dismal aspect presented itself on all sides.

For the last three days no grain had been served out in the garrison; but as many of the soldiers had been provident in times of plenty to save from their respective allowances, there existed no real want of that article in the camp, and salt and sugar were still to be had in great abundance. A small quantity of wheat still remained, which Mr. Thomas humanely appropriated to the use of the sick and wounded. The scarcity of provisions operated more severely upon the Hindoo than the Moossulman soldiers, as the latter could subsist upon the cattle that were daily destroyed by the enemy's shot.

A body of Rohillas, who were stationed in the posts that commanded the water used for the supply of the camp, suddenly went over to the enemy. Mr. Thomas instantly appointed others to guard the posts thus abandoned; but to his sorrow soon found that the spirit of desertion had seized on the Moossulman troops in general, the cavalry alone excepted. At ſeven o'clock in the evening information was brought that the whole of the troops ſtationed at the out-poſts of the camp had deſerted; that the enemy were making preparations for a general aſſault; and at the inſtant of receiving this intelligence, Mr. Thomas had the additional mortification to perceive the laſt ſtack of his hay in flames by the incendiaries. This, as it afterwards appeared, was a preconcerted ſignal between the enemy and the traitors in his own camp.

Diſtreſſed at this intelligence, Mr. Thomas demanded of the perſon who informed him wherefore he had ſo long delayed the communication; but received in reply only a vague and unſatisfactory excuſe. The ſcene of treachery now began to diſcloſe itſelf.

Shortly after Mr. Thomas's hircarrahs brought word that Shah Tab Khan, who commanded George Ghur, had already mounted his horſe, attended by his people and all their effects, and was preparing to leave the fort, being at that inſtant in conference with a party of the enemy, who had approached the walls with a determination to escort the traitor to their own camp.

His escape was easily effected, Mr. Thomas being in no condition to punish him; and on his departure, a party from camp was ordered to take possession of the fort; but by the desertion of Shah Tab Khan the face of affairs was altered considerably for the worse. The matchlock men were now deserting the camp in crowds and in all directions; a few of the officers of the whole regiment being the only persons who remained.

Mr. Thomas's sole reliance was now on the attachment of the regiment which had been commanded by the gallant but unfortunate Mr. Hopkins, at the commencement of the campaign. It was seven hundred strong; but during the late severe service had been reduced to one third of the original number. "These "(says Mr. Thomas, in the bitterness of his "anguish, occasioned by so many desertions) "were the only men that stood true to my "interests."

But even with this force, though comparatively ſo inſignificant, had there been proviſions and forage in the place, he might ſtill have defended the fort of George Ghur; but excepting the ſmall portion allotted for the ſuſtenance of the ſick and wounded men, not a ſeer of rice or grain could be procured; to complete their diſtreſs, the enemy, perceiving their forlorn ſituation, prepared to advance and overwhelm them with numbers; nothing now remained for Mr. Thomas but to attempt a retreat, and, if poſſible, carry into effect his former determination of throwing himſelf into Hanſi.

Agreeably to this determination, having ordered the cavalry to hold themſelves in readineſs, he about nine o'clock in the evening quitted his camp.

Not long after, he fell in with a party of the enemy, who attacked him with vigour: his men, diſheartened by the late events, having loſt their accuſtomed ſpirit, gave way on all ſides, and he was compelled with a few followers to fly for his life.

The enemy continuing the purſuit, he was compelled to make a circuitous route in order to avoid falling in with ſtraggling parties, by which means, though Hanſi was not more than forty coſs from George Ghur, he was compelled to travel nearly double that diſtance.*

Arrived at length in ſafety at Hanſi, Mr. Thomas's firſt care was directed to its defence.†

* In this retreat Mr. Thomas rode a favourite Persian horse of a very superior breed and the highest spirit. On this generous animal, without allowing any intermission on the road, he performed a journey of one hundred and twenty miles within twenty-four hours. This horse, which Mr. Thomas brought with him down the country, is now in the possession of Sir Frederick Hamilton, Bart. of Benares.

† Hansi, according to the Ayeen Akberi, is included in the Soobah of Delhi. Speaking of the rivers contained within this Soobah, the author of the Ayeen Akberi observes, "There are also many lesser streams, and amongst "them the Kenkkar, vulg. (Cuggur). Hansi is an ancient "city, where reposes Sheik Jumal, successor of Sheik Fe-"reed Shuker Gunj (of whom we have spoken in our de-"tail of the Battee country). The city of Hissar was "founded by Sultaun Ferose, who dug a canal which

Warned by paſt experience of the treacherous diſpoſition of the Mooſſulmans, he committed the charge of the fort and city to his faithful Rajepoots, whom on all occaſions, and in the moſt trying ſituations, he had ever found worthy his confidence.

He was not miſtaken in his conjectures, as daily inſtances occurred during the ſiege of the inconſtancy and treachery of the others.

Two pieces of artillery were all that remained in the fort fit for ſervice. The dilatory march of the enemy to inveſt the town afforded Mr. Thomas ſufficient time to caſt and mount eight additional cannon. The enemy advancing by eaſy ſtages poſſeſſed themſelves of the wells in the neighbourhood of Hanſi, and at length commenced the ſiege.

" brings the water of the Jumna near this city. This ca-
" nal passes the town of Sersah. Hissar has very few ri-
" vers, and in order to make wells, the inhabitants are
" obliged to dig to a great depth."—See Mr. Gladwin's Translation of the Ayeen Akberi, Calcutta edition—article Delhi, vol. ii.

The Rajepoots who ſtill adhered to Mr. Thomas, by this time reduced in their numbers to three hundred men, were ſtationed within the fort; the remainder of his force, conſiſting of about nine hundred men, were diſtributed for the defence of the city and the out-poſts. Aware of his very critical ſituation, Mr. Thomas himſelf remained within the fort, taking care to keep a ſtrict guard during the night.

The troops deſtined for the ſecurity of the out-poſts had ſcarcely occupied their reſpective ſtations, when, in a manner moſt daſtardly and treacherous, they delivered them over to the enemy; and the fort and city were thus left to be defended by a handſul of men.

This even was rendered impracticable by the treachery of ſome Rohillas, who invited the enemy to advance to the attack. The aſſault was accordingly made: on the entrance of the enemy into the town, a deſperate conflict was maintained on either ſide, Mr. Thomas's remaining troops fighting with the moſt determined valour: three different times the enemy were repulſed with loſs, but numbers at length prevailing, Mr. Thomas could no longer persuade his men to continue the conflict; he was therefore reluctantly compelled to take shelter within the fort, and abandon the town, of which the enemy took immediate possession.

Of his whole force, seven hundred men now only remained. The enemy having erected their batteries, commenced the siege of the fort, which, notwithstanding its siege and the small garrison which it contained, had there been a sufficiency of provisions, could still have made a successful resistance; but provisions were scarce, the Mahomedan troops were clamorous for their pay, and receiving no satisfactory answer on this head, they made offers to Mr. Perron of joining his army on condition of payment of their arrears, and an advance of money as a reward for their treachery.

Mr. Perron would readily have agreed to this proposal, had he not conceived Mr. Thomas could still defend the place with his remaining Rajepoots, in which case he might lose many of his own men; he accordingly made Mr. Thomas acquainted with the treachery that was carrying on within the garrifon, and advifed him to be upon his guard.

" Confidering, therefore, (concludes Mr. " Thomas) that I had entirely loft my party, " and with it the hopes of at prefent fubduing " my enemies, the Seiks and the powers in " the French interefts; that I had no expec- " tation of fuccour from any quarter, Luck- " wah having gone to Joudpore; that if hofti- " lities continued, my refource in money would " have failed; in this fituation, I agreed to " evacuate the fort; and the neceffary arrange- " ments being completed, I ftipulated for a " battalion of fepoys to efcort me to the Eng- " lifh frontier, where I arrived in the middle " of January, 1802.

DEATH AND CHARACTER

OF

GEORGE THOMAS.

NOT long after his arrival on the Britiſh frontier, Mr. Thomas inſpected his affairs; and on collecting the wreck of his fortune, acquired with ſo much toil and labour, he found himſelf poſſeſſed of a ſum not more than ſufficient to procure the comforts of life in his native country; with this he determined to retire from public life to the enjoyment of domeſtic eaſe and quiet; and with this intention was proceeding to Calcutta, when death arreſted his progreſs, near the military cantonments of Berhampoor, on the 22d of Auguſt, 1802. He was interred in the burying-ground of that place, and a monument is now erecting to his memory.

George Thomas was a native of Tipperary, in Ireland, about forty-ſix years of age, tall in his perſon (being upwards of ſix feet in height) and of a proportionate ſtrength of body; his countenance was bold and erect; but from the conſtant and active uſe of his limbs, during his long and arduous warfare, he had contracted an elevation of the head which gave him the appearance of ſtiffneſs; though in conſequence of this elevation his look was more martial, and indicative of the intrepidity of ſpirit which reigned within, and which wholly poſſeſſed his mind to the laſt hour of his life.

Mr. Thomas appeared formed by nature to execute the boldeſt deſigns; and though uncultivated* by education, he poſſeſſed a native and

* On his first arrival at Benares, after having obligingly promised his Excellency the Marquis Wellesley to afford every information within his power of the state of the western countries, Mr. Thomas proposed to the compiler of these memoirs to deliver his information in the Persian language; adding, that from constant use it was become more familiar to him than his native tongue. This offer, for obvious reasons, was declined; but it proves Mr. Thomas's capacity, under every disadvantage arising from a want of regular education; and I have no hesitation in declaring my opinion, that if Mr. Thomas had found leisure to cultivate his mind, his progress in the most useful

inherent vigour of mind, which qualified him for the performance of great actions, and placed him on a level with diſtinguiſhed officers of the preſent day.

That he poſſeſſed ſuperior military talents has, we truſt, been evinced by the relation of the tranſactions in the preceding pages; and in reviewing his conduct, during a long and multifarious warfare, a more competent eſtimate may perhaps be formed of his abilities, if we reflect on the nature and extent of one of his plans, which he detailed to the compiler of theſe memoirs during his reſidence at Benares. When fixed in his reſidence at Hanſi, he firſt conceived, and would, if unforeſeen and untoward circumſtances had not occurred, have executed the bold deſign of extending his conqueſts to the mouths of the Indus. This was to have been effected by a fleet of boats, conſtructed from timber procured in the foreſts near the city of Feroſepoor, on the banks of the Sutledge river, of

branches of literature would have been surprisingly rapid. He spoke, wrote, and read the Hindoostany and Persian languages with uncommon fluency and precision.

proceeding down that river with his army, and ſettling the countries he might ſubdue on his route: a daring enterpriſe, and conceived in the true ſpirit of an ancient Roman. On the concluſion of this deſign it was his intention to turn his arms againſt the Punjaub, which he expected to reduce in the courſe of a couple of years; and which, conſidering the wealth he would then have acquired, and the amazing reſources he would have poſſeſſed, theſe ſucceſſes combined would doubtleſs have contributed to eſtabliſh his authority on a firm and ſolid baſis.

Apprehenſive, however, of the ultimate ſucceſs of his arms, when he conſidered the number and ſtrength of his enemies, Mr. Thomas, about the time he was occupied in the contemplation of the aforementioned plan, made an offer* of his ſervice to the Britiſh government; which, though circumſtances of political conſideration might not have inclined govern-

* Correspondence with Captain H. V. White, to whom the compiler begs leave to offer his kindest acknowledgments for several interesting anecdotes in the latter part of Mr. Thomas's career.

ment to adopt, is nevertheless sufficient to present a correct idea of the enterprising spirit of the man. Having offered to advance and take possession of the Punjaub, and give up his army to the direction and control of the English; to take the country, and, in short, to become an active partisan in their cause: he thus, in a patriotic and truly loyal strain, concludes his remarks on the interesting subject: "* By this "plan," says he, "I have nothing in view but "the welfare of my king and country. It could "not be concerted soon enough to be of any "use in the approaching conflict; (his dispute "with the Mahrattas); therefore it is not to "better myself that I have thought of it; I "shall be sorry to see my conquests fall to the "Mahrattas, I wish to give them to my king, "and to serve him the remainder of my days; "and this I can only do as a soldier in this part "of the world."

His knowledge of the spirit and character of the different tribes and nations that compose the interior of the vast peninsula of India,

* Captain White's correspondence.

was various, extenſive, and correct; and no man perhaps ever more thoroughly ſtudied, or more properly appreciated, the Indian character at large. In his manners he was gentle and inoffenſive, and poſſeſſed a natural politeneſs, and evinced a diſpoſition to pleaſe ſuperior to moſt men. He was, as we have already ſeen, equally a loyal ſubject to his king, as a real and ſincere well wiſher to the proſperity and permanence of the Britiſh empire in the eaſt. He was open, generous, charitable, and humane; and his behaviour towards the families of thoſe perſons who fell in his ſervice, evinces a benevolence of heart, and a philanthropy of ſpirit, highly honourable to his character.

But with theſe good qualities, the impartiality of hiſtory demands that we ſhould ſtate his errors, and endeavour to diſcover ſome ſhades in a character otherwiſe ſplendid. A quickneſs of temper, liable to frequent agitations, and the ebullitions of haſty wrath, not unfrequently rendered his appearance ferocious; yet this only occurred in inſtances where the conviviality of his temper obſcured his reaſon; and for this, on conviction, no man was ever readier to make every acknowledgment and reparation in his power.

Perfect correctneſs of conduct cannot be expected from a character like the one now under conſideration, as a ſecluſion from civilized life, and long abſence from the exerciſe of thoſe duties which conſtitute the chief enjoyment of ſocial happineſs, muſt neceſſarily have tinctured the manners of the man with ſome portion of the ſpirit of the barbarians with whom he was ſo long an inmate.

Upon the whole, however, we may be juſtified in remarking, that on a review of the life and actions of this very extraordinary man, it is difficult which moſt to admire, whether the intrepidity of ſpirit by which he was incited to the performance of actions which, by their effect, raiſed him from the condition of a private ſubject to rank and diſtinction among princes; or the wonderful and uncommon attachment generally exhibited towards his perſon and intereſts, by natives of every deſcription, who fought and conquered with him in his long and arduous career, and whoſe aſſiſtance exalted him for a time to a height of reſpectability and conſequence that ſeldom falls to the lot of an individual.

FINIS.

CONTENTS OF THE APPENDIX.

APPENDIX I.

Of the Trade in general carried on in the Countries to the North-Weſt of Delhi.

I. PUNJAUB.

AN open trade with this country from every part of Hindooſtan has long ſince ceaſed; but petty merchants, by applying for paſſports from the reſpective chiefs of the Seik territories, previous to entering their boundaries, are generally ſupplied with them, and by this means ſtill continue a trifling commercial intercourſe.

Their exports to the countries weſt of the Attock, conſiſt of ſugar, rice, indigo, wheat, and white cloth. Their imports from thoſe countries are ſwords, horſes, fruit, lead, and ſpices. Their exports to Caſhmere may be confidered nearly the fame as into Perfia ; their imports from Cafhmere are fhawls, and a variety of cloths, faffron, and fruit.

With the inhabitants of the mountains they exchange cloth, matchlocks, and horfes, for iron, and other inferior commodities. From the Deckan are imported fulphur, indigo, falt, lead, iron, Europe coarfe cloth, and fpices: their exports are horfes, camels, fugar, rice, white cloth, matchlocks, fwords, and bows and arrows.

This trade is not carried on by any particular route, but depends on the character of the chiefs of thofe diftricts through which they pafs. The moft confiderable part of the trade is, however, carried on from Amrut Seer, by way of Machaywara, to Duttyala; fouthward by way of Hanfi, Rauge Ghur, and Oreecha, into the weftern part of the Rajepoot country by way of Kythul Jeind, and Dadery, and finally by Karnaul towards Delhi and the Ganges.

II. BATTIES.

The exports of the Batties, conſiſt of horſes, camels, bullocks, buffaloes, and ghee; their imports are coarſe white cloth, ſugar, and ſalt; but the trade is very inconſiderable, and is carried on by petty merchants of Bahadra, Noher, and other towns, through the means of the diſciples of Shiekh Fereed. The Hiſar, or Harriana diſtricts import matchlocks, ſwords, coarſe white cloth, ſalt, ſugar, a ſmall quantity of rice, wheat, and ſpices, their exports are horſes, camels, bullocks, and ghee.

III. BEYKANEER.

Beykaneer imports coarſe and fine rice, ſugar, opium, and indigo. The former articles they import from the Punjaub and by Rauge Ghur and Churoo; ſalt they get from Samber, and wheat from the Jypoor country; ſpices, copper, and coarſe cloth, from Jeſſelmere. They have no exports but cattle, and thoſe are of an inferior breed.

IV. JOUDPOOR.

The country of Joudpoor imports iron, copper, cloth of different ſorts, red and yellow broad cloth, rice, opium, ſugar, and ſpices. The copper and broad cloth are brought from Surat, from Tatta on the Indus, and from the Jypoor and Mewar countries.

Rice, ſugar, and wheat from Mewar, Goorwara, and the ſouthern parts of their own country.

Their exports are horſes, bullocks, and camels, of ſuperior ſize, which are in great requeſt in various parts of India; ſalt likewiſe from the Sambre lake, and other places in its vicinity, is exported to the Punjaub to the eaſt and to the ſouth.

The trade to this country from Surat, paſſes chiefly through Gujerath and Ahumdabad; from Tatta through the Sindy country and Jeſſelmere, and to the Deckan, by Mewar and Kota.

The town of Pawley is the greateſt mart in this part of Rajepootana; for there the merchants exchange the commodities of Europe, Perſia, and Deckan, for thoſe of Caſhmere, Punjaub, and Hindooſtan.

The trade in moſt parts of the Rajepoot country is carried on by camels or bullocks; this is unavoidable, the ſandineſs of the ſoil rendering it almoſt impaſſable to carriages.

V. KOTA AND BOONDY.

The produce of Mewar, Kota, and Boondy, the eaſtern parts of the dominions of Jypoor, and the diſtricts poſſeſſed by the rajah of Karoolee, may be mentioned under the following heads: horſes, camels, and other cattle, but inferior to thoſe produced in the more weſtern countries; matchlocks, ſwords, cloth of a coarſe manufacture, wheat, rice, ſugar, chuna, barley, and all other Indian grain; and though about fourteen or fifteen coſs north of the city of Oudipoor ſulphur is produced, it is inferior to that which comes from Surat.

From the abundant production of thofe countries, a perfon would naturally think the inhabitants were in want of few importations; but they are extravagant in their mode of living, and fond of foreign luxuries.

Their imports and exports correfpond with thofe of Jypoor; European and Perfian articles come by the channels of Gujerath, Jefelmere, and Pawlee. From the Deckan, by way of Bapaul Soronge, Udjeen, and Endore, to Kota and Beelwara, in the Mewar diftrict.

The Ghoffeins of Nathdorah, a place twelve cofs north from the city of Oudipoor, carry on a confiderable trade with the provinces of Gujerath, and Tatta, and with Rajepootana, Punjaub, and Hindooftan.

This trade confifts of pearls, precious ftones, arms, fhawls, cloth of every fort, and in fhort the production of all nations that trade to India. Kota being in a central pofition, and the rajah a man of good character, is a place of great trade, and ſerves as a general depoſit for merchandize.

VI. JYPOOR.

The Jypoor country producing in itſelf almoſt every neceſſary article, does not ſtand in ſuch real want of foreign commodities. The rajah is in part poſſeſſor of Samber, which produces plenty of ſalt, as likewiſe do the diſtricts of Senganah and Berath. To theſe may be added copper, mines, alum, blue ſtone, and verdigriſe. There are likewiſe in moſt parts of Jypoor good cattle, though not in quality equal to thoſe of Joudpoor.

In all parts of the Jypoor dominions are manufactories of cloth, of ſwords, and of matchlocks.

Its imports are, fine cloths, the tiſſue manufactures of Benares, and ſhawls from Caſhmere. From Guzzerath and Tatta are ſupplied opium, lead, and ſheet copper; horſes and fruits from Perſia were formerly introduced by the route of Beykaneer, but at preſent the Karwans paſs through Jeſelmere, and Joudpoor. The court of Jypoor being ſplendid and luxurious, ſo is the conſumption of the productions of other countries conſiderable. This encourages trade, and leads to an intercourſe with all parts of India.

APPENDIX II.

THE following profpectus, drawn up about eleven years ago, when the compiler of thefe memoirs was employed on a furvey ordered by government through the Dooab and the countries adjacent, will exhibit to the reader the outlines of a plan, the greater part of which is now, by God's bleffing, happily accomplished.

It is here, therefore, that he wifhes to pay the tribute fo deſervedly due to the memory of that illustrious luminary, the father of oriental literature, his honoured and revered friend, Sir William Jones, whofe kind encouragement firft infpired the compiler with an ardour for eaftern literature, and whofe bright example and uncommon acquirements in every branch of polite learning, muft ever prove the beft and ftrongeft incentive to the exertions of Britifh youth.

PROSPECTUS.

Having been appointed in 1792 to accompany an efcort ordered to attend captain Reynolds, of the Bombay eftablifhment, on a furvey through the Dooab and the adjoining countries, it appears to me, that in the courfe of this expedition, much information may be gained on fubjects not hitherto fufficiently inveftigated and developed; what I conceive to be moft ufeful in the refearches above alluded to, may be reduced under the following heads:

1ft. The natural productions of the Dooab, with its commercial advantages, and a comparative view of its former and prefent revenues, with as accurate a calculation of its inhabitants as can be procured.

2nd. The places of note, and the monuments of Mahomedan grandeur fince the conqueft of the Moguls.

3d. An account of Calpee and Etyah, and of the improvements that may be made in the inland commerce with the neighbouring countries.

4th. The cities of Agra and Delhi, and their environs, notwithſtanding their preſent ruinous ſtate, will nevertheleſs yield materials for many intereſting remarks. The hiſtory of the revolutions at Delhi, and the unfortunate cataſtrophe of the preſent deſcendant of Timoor, would, I am perſuaded, be intereſting to my countrymen at home, and great and accurate information on this ſubject may be gained by perſonal converſation with ſeveral of the actors in this revolution, who are now living at Delhi.*

5th. The celebrated city of Mathura, and the plains of Bindrabund, preſent a field for the inveſtigation of the ancient government of the Hindoos; for, on this ſpot, conſecrated for ages by the ſuperſtition of their anceſtors, we may hope to find thoſe primitive manners

* See the History of Shah Aulum, and present work.

and cuſtoms deſcribed in their Sanſcrit manuſcripts; and their religious opinions being cloſely connected with their civil ordinations, we may be able to form a more correct idea of the ſpirit of their ancient government.

6th. On the ſouth and ſouth-weſt of the Jumna, the provinces of Boondeelcund, and Gohud, which have lately been reduced by the Mahratta government, with reſpect to their ſituation towards the Vizier's frontier, are objects of conſequence to the British nation, and demand an attentive inveſtigation.

7th. From the late ſucceſſes attendant on Scindiah's arms, we muſt naturally conclude it has been owing in a great degree to the attention he has paid to the internal diſcipline and economy of his military ſyſtem; it is therefore my intention to obtain as correct information as I can of the ſtate of the Marhatta armies, together with an account of the Mahratta government.*

* The late maha-rajah Madajee Scindiah.

THE SEIKS.

8th. This nation, ſo obſcure as hardly to be mentioned even as a tribe, at the beginning of the preſent century, have, within theſe laſt thirty years, raiſed themſelves in ſuch reputation as not only to attract the notice, but excite the alarm of their neighbours on both ſides of their government.

They poſſeſs the whole of the Punjaub, and it is very probable will one day or other have an eye to a participation of the Vizier's provinces. I propoſe, therefore, to obtain every poſſible information of their tribe, manners, cuſtoms, and ſpirit of government, and, ſhould we be able, to penetrate into the Punjaub, to deſcribe the face of that country, and the natural and commercial productions.*

9th. The deſiderata of Major Rennel, which from a peruſal of his moſt excellent memoir I

* See the History of Shah Aulum, and present work.

find to be, first, the ascertaining the existence of one of the grand designs of the Emperor Feroze; which was, to have cut a canal from the Sutledge to the Jumna, which would have opened a communication by water from Cabul to Assam. Major Rennel observes, he takes it for granted this canal was never completed, as no farther intimation has been obtained on that head. The remains * of such a magnificent work, if any still exist, must doubtless be discovered by an inspection on the spot.

10th. I have in my possession a history of the celebrated Timoor or Tamerlane, said to be written by himself. This work contains the whole of Timoor's expeditions, from an early period of his life until near his death. The Indian expedition in particular is detailed in a very accurate manner.

11th. THE ALTARS OF ALEXANDER.

I have been the more induced to present to the public the above prospectus, as an evidence

* See the 14th chapter of the present work.

that the leiſure allowed to officers in the hours of relaxation from their profeſſional duties, has not altogether been thrown away ; and alſo in the entertaining a confident hope that the honeſt purſuit of laudable ſtudies will ever meet with public approbation and ſupport.

APPENDIX III.

General Statement of the Forces of ſeveral of the Natives Princes and States in the weſtern Parts of the Peninſula.

THE preſent force of Dowlut Row Scindiah may be ſtated under the following heads.

1ſt. Cavalry, Marhatta, and Hindooſtany, including the cavalry ſtationed with the different collectors that might be brought to act in a war	20,000
Ambajee's cavalry in the diſtrict of Gualior	4,000
Mr. Perron might muſter in Hindooſtan, that is, Delhi, Agrah, Jauts, Bapoo Scindia, and Madhoo Row's cavalry, excluſive of Seiks or Rajepoots	7,000
Entire force of Scindiah's cavalry	31,000

Scindiah's Infantry.

2d. The number of battalions at preſent under the command of Mr. Perron amount to forty; each battalion generally conſiſts of five hundred men, gunners and fighting men of every deſcription included. Each battalion is provided with four field-pieces, a carronade, or howitzer, and ſome pieces of ordnance of large caliber, for the purpoſe of throwing grape.

A brigade conſiſts of eight battalions; it has generally a ſeparate park of ten pieces of artillery attached to it. This park is compoſed of battering guns and ſpare field-pieces.

The ſtrength of each brigade will conſiſt as follows.

Strength in officers and fighting men of every deſcription		4,150
Pieces of artillery	—	50
Strength of five brigades		20,750
Pieces of artillery	—	250

The remains of Colonel Felose's brigade, six battalions, men	3,000
Ordnance — —	60
Five battalions of Col. John Hessing	2,600
Ordnance — —	30
Ambajee's battalions may be computed at four hundred men each, of which he has sixteen battalions	6,400
His artillery is not regularly attached to his battalions, and therefore often varies; but, generally speaking, may be computed at four pieces to each battalion — —	64
The battering train likewise varies, but may be computed at pieces	20
Total artillery of Ambajee's pieces	84

Begum Somroo.

*Five battalions of about six hundred men each — —	3,000
Pieces of artillery —	24
Cavalry — —	150

* I find by this, that the statement of the Begum's force, as given in the History of Shah Aulum, is partly incorrect.

Bapooh Scindiah

Has two battalions	—	1,000
Artillery pieces	— —	10
Total force of Scindiah in cavalry		31,150
Total force in infantry		38,050
Grand total infantry and cavalry		69,200
Grand total artillery ditto pieces		518

REMARKS BY MR. THOMAS.

* It is proper to obſerve, that Mr. Perron and Ambajee are now levying troops, which may cauſe a material error in this ſtatement a few months hence. Ambajee and Perron are poſſeſſed of artillery excluſive of the above-mentioned; and Scindiah, by the artillery taken from Holkar, is able to add conſiderably to his own part.

Preſent ſtate of Scindiah's infantry. They are the worſt in India; are not commanded by

* This statement was made 1802.

officers of experience, nor well armed, nor cordially attached to the ſervice of their maſter; they are in arrears of pay, and would be defeated by a ſmall force of regular diſciplined troops, with a few pieces of well ſerved artillery.

Mr. Perron's infantry are in appearance the beſt troops belonging to Scindiah: they are under better ſubordination to their officers, and are more regularly paid, armed, clothed, and diſciplined.

The troops of the late Colonel Feloſe and thoſe of Colonel Heſſing, ore equal to thoſe of Mr. Perron.

Thoſe of Begum Somroo are in a ſtate of inſubordination, and mutinous.

Thoſe of Ambajee and Bapoo Scindia do not deſerve the name of troops; they are undiſciplined and ill-armed.

Their artillery is in general bad, and is frequently diſmounted of itſelf in the uſual course of firing in a field of battle. Mr. Thomas relates one inftance where twenty-five pieces of cannon were rendered unfit for service, eight of which only were ftruck by the enemy's fhot.

Force of Ali Behaudur.

Ali Behaudur, the Marhatta chief, who is in poffeffion of the open country, as likewife feveral of the ftrong holds in Boondeelcund, has four battalions, confifting of between five and fix thoufand infantry, fix or feven thoufand cavalry, with forty or fifty pieces of artillery, all of the very worft quality. The battalions, each about five hundred ftrong, are without difcipline, or military regulation of any kind, and may be confidered as a rabble.

The infantry confifts of Rohillas, Boondeelahs, and Malwa Sebundys, who are armed with matchlocks.

The cavalry confifts of Marhatta Mooffulmans from Cuttair, (Rohilcund) and from the Doo Ab.

The beſt troops in the intereſt of this chief are the cavalry of his aſſociate Himmut Behaudur, the Ghoſſeen; they are in number about two thouſand, and are choſen men.

Himmut Behaudur has likewiſe a body of infantry, amounting to about three thouſand. We may therefore compute the collected force of Ali Behaudur at twenty-one thouſand, chiefly rabble, and incapable, ſays Mr. Thomas, of oppoſing a regular and diſciplined force, though far inferior in point of numbers.

At the head of this rabble, theſe chiefs keep poſſeſſion of a country capable of yielding a revenue of one crore of rupees.

Detail of the force of Ali Behaudur;

four battalions, men		—	2,000
Irregular infantry ditto			6,000
Cavalry	—	—	7,000
Artillery	—	—	50

Force of Himmut Behaudur.

(In the ſervice of Ali Behaudur.)

Irregular infantry	—	—	3,000
Cavalry —	—	—	2,000
Artillery pieces	—	—	20

Combined force of Ali Behaudur and Himmut Behaudur.

Cavalry	—	—	9,000
Infantry,	—	—	11,000
To which may be added infantry attached to the guns	—	—	1,000
		Grand total, men	21,000
Pieces of artillery	—	—	70

Preſent Force of Kaſhi Row Holkar, and Jeſſwunt Row Holkar.

The cavalry of theſe two chiefs may be computed at thirty thouſand, excluſive of the Pindaries or irregular horſe. In this ſtatement, made from information received from writers and ſoldiers in their ſervice, who ſeldom fail to add to the number, there may probably be ſome error. But it is certain that Jeſſwunt Row Holkar is actually at the head of a body of cavalry amounting to twenty thouſand men; Kaſhi Row Holkar has from four to five thouſand cavalry at Indore, his capital; to which, if the cavalry of Ameer Khaun, a tributary, be added, as likewiſe that under the different collectors, the number will amount in the aggregate to thirty thouſand. Theſe chiefs occaſionally receive the aid of from ſix to ten thouſand Pindaries, a banditti who lay waſte the countries through which they paſs, by predatory warfare.

Force in Infantry.

Conſiſting of eight battalions computed at four hundred men per battalion, — —	3,200
Artillery men, —	600
Rohillas, — —	10,000
Total infantry	13,800
Artillery pieces —	50

Holkar's cavalry are ſuperior to thoſe of Scindiah, being better officered, and more correſpondent with the real Mahratta cuſtom of predatory warfare.

The infantry (obſerves Mr. Thomas) are very bad. They are ill paid, badly officered, and without ſubordination; undiſciplined, nor can they make uſe of their arms in action.

The Rohillas in Holkar's ſervice are a faithleſs rabble, who will ſtand true only as long as they find it their intereſt; they are always ready to leave or ruin him, if not regularly paid; or when expected to move againſt an enemy of ſuperior force; or if by any means they ſhould have accumulated money.

Detailed Statement of the collected Force of Kaſhi Row Holkar, and Jeſſwunt Row Holkar.

Cavalry, — —	30,000
Pindaries or Looties, mounted on ſmall horſes, — —	10,000
Total cavalry,	40,000

Infantry.

Eight battalions at four hundred men each, — —	3,200
Artillery men, &c. —	600
Rohillas, — —	10,000
Total infantry,	13,100
Artillery pieces, — —	60
Grand total,	53,800

APPENDIX IV.

A general Abstract of the Countries, and their Inhabitants in the north-west parts of the Peninsula af Hindoostan; with the Distance of the capital Cities from Delhi in British Miles.

1st. THE Punjuab or country of the Seiks, is composed of the province of Lahore, and the chukla or division called Sirhind. The inhabitants in general are Seiks, though the cultivators of the soil are many of them Jauts.

Force. Cavalry 60,000. Artillery 40 pieces. Infantry 5,000. Revenue 5 crores.

Capital, Lahore, N. W. by N. three hundred miles.

2d. The Hurrianah country is included in the Sirkar of Hiſſar; it is called in the map the Leſſer Baloochiſtaun. The inhabitants are chiefly Jauts, with the exception of a few Rajepoot, and Rungur villages, which laſt appellation is given to ſuch of the Rajepoots who have embraced the Mahomedan religion. Does not Rungur imply coloured, or ſtained, or of mixed blood?

Capital, Hiſſar, W. N. W. one hundred and eight miles.

3d. The country called Tahneſſar conſiſts of the weſtern parts of Tahneſſar, Kernaul, Kythul, Panniput, Sefeedoo, Jeind, Koſohan, and Dehatarut. The inhabitants are chiefly Jauts, though ſome have become Seiks, and a few are Rajepoots, but of a low caſt.

No particular capital.

4th. The Battee country; the chiefs of which are Rajepoot Mooſſulmans; the common people are Jauts who have become Mooſſulmans, and the cultivators of the ſoil are termed Ryis, and are a peaceable inoffensive race.

Capital, Batnier, W. N. W. two hundred and nineteen miles.

5th. Beykaneer is governed by Rathore Rajepoots; the cultivators are Jauts.

Force. Cavalry 2,000. Artillery 30 pieces.
Infantry 3,000. Revenue 5 lacks.

Capital, Beykaneer.

6th. The Jypoor country is governed by Rajepoots of the Kutchwa tribe; the cultivators are Jauts, Bremins and Meenas.

Cavalry 30,000. Artillery 40 pieces.
Infantry 10,000. Revenue 60 lacks.

Capital Jypoor or Jynaghur, S. W. one hundred and fifty miles.

7th The Row Rajah is a Rathore Rajepoot;

the cultivators of his country are Jauts Mewattes, and Aheers, a savage tribe, approaching in their manners to the Jauts.

Cavalry	1,500.	Artillery	16 pieces.
Infantry	2,000.	Revenue	6 lacks.

Capital Alwur,* S. W. by S. 90 miles.

* This place, the fort of which is situated on the summit of a high hill, is thus described in a work published some years since by Elias Habesci, but better known to the English reader under the name of Count Gika. "The "emperors had likewise kept Aloor, a country very fertile "in mines, and not at a great distance from Mattra. On "those mountains there is another distinct nation called "Mina, whose most splendid quality is that they excel all "others in stealing, and we are assured that they are the "most dexterous pilferers of India. They are capable of "carrying off a horse or a prisoner from the most vigilant "guard. All these countries produce infinite quantities "of cattle, in which their principal trade consists.

"The richest, most agreeable, and most commodious "place in those parts is the plain or valley of Tannagasi, "two leagues in length and one in breadth, which contains "now seventeen mines that are opened, and as they are "well explored, they may be reckoned to produce a crore "of rupees annually. The province of Aloar is dependant "on Jypoor, or should be. It is in general as fertile in "mines as the other, and is rich; but the little province

8th. Joudpoor, whose ruler is called the Rhathore Rajah and Marwar Rajah. He is a

" of Tannagasi, which is subject to Aloar, is really the " most substantial part. Tannagasi lies at only four days " small journies from Mattra. The capital and only town " bears the same name. It is pretty large, trades consi- " derably, and is situated at the foot of a mountain, on " which there is a fort, with some pieces of artillery. In " 1780 and 1781, a Frenchman commanding the artillery " of Nadjifkan undermined this garrison; but it surren- " dered before the mine was sprung.

" If the English chose to seize on Aloar and Tannagasi, " their army, which I suppose to be encamped at Mattra, " must march to Deeg in a single day. Proceeding thence " they should leave Aloa ten English miles to the right: " they would find no opposition hitherto. It is only at " Sakmin Ghur that we find a fort, which commands the " plain that leads to a pass on the road to Tannagasi. At " that pass there is another small fort, and both together " could not hold out twenty-four hours against an attack " in form. Tannagasi is the terrestrial paradise of that " country: it is there that decent employment would be " found for two hundred individuals of the English nation; " and, aided by two battalions, they would be enabled to " explore peaceably all its mines, and make them produce " sixty lacks of rupees, clear of all expences, in each year: " but in the case two redoubts should be constructed on " the two banks of the Jumna to protect the passage-boats " for merchandize and minerals, they might send from " Tannagasi, escorted by a company of the battalions that

Rhathore Rajepoot of the pureſt and moſt ancient blood of the Rajepoots. The cultivators are Jauts.

Cavalry	27,000.	Artillery	30 pieces.
Infantry	3,000.	Revenue	20 lacks.

Capital Joudpoor, S. W. by W. 350 miles.

9th. Karolee, whoſe Rajah is of the tribe of Rajepoot, called Jadoo. The cultivators are Jauts, Bramins, and Meenas.

Cavalry	6,000.	Artillery	12 pieces.
Infantry	2,000.	Revenue	5 lacks.

Capital Karolee, ſouth 140 miles.

10th. The Kiſhen Ghur Rajah is of the tribe of Rhathore Rajepoots. The cultivators are Jauts.

" would be stationed there. From Mattra the goods might " pass on to Futty Ghur, or some other place on the " Ganges, to be sent thence to a greater distance. The " navigation of the Jumna as far as Allahabad might be " attempted."——See Objects interesting to the English Nation, vol. ii. page 113 and 114, Calcutta edition, A. D. 1793.

Capital Kifhen Ghur, S. W. by W. 200 miles.

11th. Oudipoor or Mewar, whofe ruler is called likewife the Ranah of Chittore, from the celebrated fort of that name fituated within his dominions. Confult Colonel Dow's Hiftory of Hindooftan. This prince is alfo called Urfee Rannah, which was affumed by one of his anceftors, and adopted by his fucceffors. He is of the tribe called Sefodiah. The cultivators of Oudipoor are compofed of Rajepoots, Jauts, Bramins, and Beils.

Cavalry	12,000
Infantry	6,000

Capital Oudipoor, S. W. 350 miles.

12th. The principalities of Kota and Boondee, whofe chiefs are of the Chohan tribe, and are likewife denominated Addah Rajepoots. The cultivators are Rajepoots, Jauts, Bramins, Beels, and other claffes.

Force. Infantry 2,000

Cavalry	3,000
Artillery	20 pieces.
Revenue	30 lacks.

Capital Kota and Boondee, S. W. 250 miles.

13th. The Burtpoor Rajah is a Jaut, the cultivators are chiefly Jauts.*.

Force,	Cavalry	1,000
	Infantry	2,000
	Artillery	20 pieces.
	Revenue	15 lacks.

Capital Burtpoor, ſouth 100 miles.

* Of this ſingular tribe, the ingenious author of Objects interesting to the English Nation thus remarks:—" The " Jattes derive their origin from a ſingle head of a family, " whose name was Ram-gee; he had thirty-four children, " who gave him many grand-children, who all respected " him as their father and prince. The eldest of the fa- " mily in direct line has always been acknowledged as " Ram-gee himself; they were cultivators; thence their " attachment to agriculture. They remained in obscurity " until the fall of the Mogul empire; they have seized on " Agra, and extended their power as far as Siren, on the " road to Lahore. Their chiefs resided at Agra with the " title of Rajah's; the first of them that acquired repu- " tation was named Jonas Sing; his successor's name was

" Creten Sing, and that of the last chief was Naval Sing. " Since this nation has been defeated by Nadjuf Khan, " it has fallen into contempt and oblivion; for they " have loſt their conquests, and are now confined " to Burtpoor, which is the capital of their little " country; but it is very strong, its ditches are of a " breadth more than is usual elsewhere, they are fifty-six " feet deep, and are always filled with water that comes " from a perennial spring. Their present chief, who now " retains the title of Rajah, is called Rengit Sing, who is " at the same time the chief of their religion, which is that " of the Hindoos."——See Objects interesting to the English Nation, vol. ii. p. 120 and 121.

CONCLUSION.

IN the force above detailed, a ſtatement of the militia of the country is not included; their numbers are conſiderable, and they in fact conſtitute the chief ſupport of their reſpective ſtates.

Under the head revenue, that which is paid into the treaſury of each prince is here deſignated; the revenue ariſing from lands granted to the different chiefs in Jaiedad, is not included in any ſtate, excepting in the Punjaub, as more fully explained in our account of that country.

By the artillery here mentioned, is only meant what is capable of being brought into the field, few of which are in good order; ſome of the chiefs have a numerous artillery in their ſorts, to which however they pay but little attention.

Conſidering the ſurpriſing fertility of ſoil, the abundance of all things neceſſary for the ſupport of the inhabitants, and the internal riches of theſe countries, and their capability of improvement, as well in regard to commercial as political relations, it is matter of no ſmall ſurpriſe to think they ſhould for ſo long a time have remained almoſt unknown to the British nation in India; and that, after being ſovereigns of ſo conſiderable a part of this extenſive empire, we ſhould now, for the firſt time, receive information, that the faireſt part of the country is yet unknown to us.

This however is the fact, and it would appear that Great Britain might derive conſiderable advantages from a cloſer alliance and more intimate acquaintance with the countries in the interior parts of India; and more eſpecially with the Rajepoot ſtates. Theſe countries, as well from the advantages of natural ſituation as from their immenſe internal refources, would be able to form the ftrongeft barrier againft the entrance of our political rivals, the French, to the central parts of the peninfula, whenever a renewal of hoftilities may induce the attempt.

POSTSCRIPT.

The compiler of these Memoirs has particular pleasure in delivering to his readers a letter lately received from an Officer of rank in the service of Scindiah, respecting Mr. Thomas's character, and which comes in a manner more peculiarly appropriate, as being the genuine effusions of a liberal mind, and the honourable testimony of a gentleman who, though an enemy from necessity, has, for the sake of justice alone, paid the tribute which he thought due to Mr. Thomas's merits as a man and a soldier.

DEAR SIR,

I AM happy to learn, from the public prints, that we are soon to have the pleasure of a life of the late George Thomas, from your pen; as he was a singular character, which deserves to be rescued from oblivion, and as I was intimately acquainted with him, and was principally employed by General Perron, to perſuade him to enter with his troops into the ſervice of Scindia. Moreover being concerned in arranging the capitulation of Hanſi, after he had the misfortune to loſe his army, and in conducting him to the British frontier; if you think I can ſupply any facts, or offer any materials which might elucidate or add to the work, I ſhall be not only happy, but proud to contribute all in my power.

I had a ſincere reſpect for his character; I regretted his misfortunes, and I did all in my power to obviate those misfortunes by my advice and my conduct; all my influence with General Perron was exerted to ſerve him, and I did every thing in my power to meliorate the ſeverity of his misfortunes, after he had been unfortunate from the doubtful event of war; and I ſhould be happy if I could afford the ſmalleſt matter towards the record of his fame. With ſome oddities, and many ſingularities, he was an uncommon character; and his exertion towards ſtation, power, riches, and glory, were ſtill more uncommon; he was uncommonly ambitious, which was the principal cauſe that led to his ruin; he would be all or nothing. To ſerve under the orders of another was an inglorious dependance, in his eſtimation of things; and the diſtraction which then prevailed in Scindiah's government, offered an enticing field to diſplay his courage and his abilities; for courage he poſſeſſed in an eminent degree; and he certainly had abilities, if a clear head, a ſolid judgment, and acute diſcernment, may be called by that name. Hoping you will pardon this intruſion, and view it in the light in which it is intended, to add my mite to tranſmit the name of George Thomas to poſterity, ſuffer me to remain with eſteem,

Dear Sir,

Your moſt obedient ſervant,

LEWIS F. SMITH.

Burhanpore,
18*th July*, 1803.